Roger G. Ibbotson
Yale School of Management
Zebra Capital Management

Moshe A. Milevsky
Schulich School of Business, York University
IFID Centre

Peng Chen, CFA
Ibbotson Associates

Kevin X. Zhu
Ibbotson Associates

Lifetime Financial Advice: Human Capital, Asset Allocation, and Insurance

RESEARCH FOUNDATION
OF CFA INSTITUTE

Statement of Purpose

The Research Foundation of CFA Institute is a
not-for-profit organization established to promote
the development and dissemination of relevant
research for investment practitioners worldwide.

The Research Foundation of CFA Institute and the Research Foundation logo are trademarks owned by The Research Foundation of CFA Institute. CFA®, Chartered Financial Analyst®, AIMR-PPS®, and GIPS® are just a few of the trademarks owned by CFA Institute. To view a list of CFA Institute trademarks and a Guide for the Use of CFA Institute Marks, please visit our website at www.cfainstitute.org.

This publication is designed to provide accurate and authoritative information in regard to the subject matter covered. It is sold with the understanding that the publisher is not engaged in rendering legal, accounting, or other professional service. If legal advice or other expert assistance is required, the services of a competent professional should be sought.

ISBN 978-0-943205-94-6

6 April 2007

Editorial Staff

Elizabeth A. Collins
Book Editor

David L. Hess
Assistant Editor

Kara H. Morris
Production Manager

Lois Carrier
Production Specialist

Lifetime Financial Advice: Human Capital, Asset Allocation, and Insurance

Biographies

Roger G. Ibbotson is a professor at the Yale School of Management and chairman of Zebra Capital Management, a quantitative equity hedge fund manager. In addition, he is founder of and adviser to Ibbotson Associates, now a Morningstar, Inc., company. He has written numerous books and articles, including the annually updated *Stocks, Bonds, Bills, and Inflation* (with Rex Sinquefield), which serves as a standard reference for information on capital market returns. He taught for many years at the University of Chicago, where he also served as executive director of the Center for Research in Security Prices. Professor Ibbotson has earned many awards for his writing, including several Graham and Dodd Scroll Awards from the *Financial Analysts Journal*. He received his bachelor's degree in mathematics from Purdue University, his MBA from Indiana University, and his PhD from the University of Chicago.

Moshe A. Milevsky is an associate professor of finance at the Schulich School of Business, York University, and the executive director of the IFID Centre in Toronto. Professor Milevsky has written five books and published more than 45 articles on the topics of investments, insurance, and pensions. He is currently the co-editor of the *Journal of Pension Economics and Finance* and is a monthly columnist for *Research Magazine*. He has consulted and lectured widely on the topic of retirement income planning and is currently a member of the Bank of Montreal Financial Group Advisory Council on Retirement and a member of the Fidelity Institute External Advisory Board. In the summer of 2002, he was designated a fellow of the Fields Institute for Research in Mathematical Sciences. He has a PhD in business finance, an MA in mathematics and statistics, and a BA in mathematics and physics.

Peng Chen, CFA, is president and chief investment officer at Ibbotson Associates, a registered investment adviser and wholly owned subsidiary of Morningstar, Inc. He has played a key role in the development of Ibbotson's investment consulting and 401(k) advice/managed retirement account services. A respected researcher, Dr. Chen has expertise in asset allocation, portfolio risk measurement, nontraditional assets, and global financial markets. His writings have appeared in the *Financial Analysts Journal, Journal of Portfolio Management, Journal of Investing, Journal of Financial Planning, Bank Securities Journal, American Association of Individual Investors Journal, Consumer Interest Annual,* and *Journal of Financial Counseling and Planning*. He received the Articles of Excellence Award from the Certified Financial Planner Board in 1996 and a 2003 Graham and Dodd Scroll Award from the *Financial Analysts Journal*. Dr. Chen received his bachelor's degree in industrial management engineering from Harbin Institute of Technology and his master's and doctorate in consumer economics from Ohio State University.

Kevin X. Zhu is a senior research consultant at Ibbotson Associates, a Morningstar, Inc., company. His research covers such areas as asset allocation coupled with human capital and/or insurance products, portfolio construction, investment strategies, mutual fund performance and selection, and personal finance. Dr. Zhu also contributes to the development of various Ibbotson products and methodologies, including software, investment management services, and retirement income solutions. His writings have appeared in the *Financial Analysts Journal*. Dr. Zhu received his doctorate in finance and master's degree in economics from York University. He received his bachelor's degree in mathematics from Lanzhou University.

Acknowledgments

We would like to thank the Research Foundation of CFA Institute for its support in making this monograph possible. We especially appreciate the assistance, support, and encouragement of Research Director Larry Siegel. We also want to acknowledge Michael Henkel, Thomas Idzorek, Sherman Hanna, Jin Wang, Huaxiong Huang, and Robert Kreitler for many helpful discussions regarding some of the underpinnings of this work. We would also like to acknowledge the assistance provided by research associates and staff at the IFID Centre and Ibbotson Associates. Finally, we want to thank Alexa Auerbach and the editorial staff members of CFA Institute for extensive editing assistance.

Contents

PROFESSIONAL
DEVELOPMENT
QUALIFIED ACTIVITY

This publication qualifies for 5 PD credits under the guidelines
of the CFA Institute Professional Development Program.

Foreword

Life-cycle finance is arguably the most important specialty in finance. At some level, all institutions exist to serve the individual. But investing directly by individuals, who reap the rewards of their successes and suffer the consequences of their mistakes, is becoming a dramatically larger feature of the investment landscape. In such circumstances, designing institutions and techniques that allow ordinary people to save enough money to someday retire—or to achieve other financial goals—is self-evidently a worthwhile effort, but until now, researchers have devoted too little attention to it.

The central problem of life-cycle finance is the spreading of the income from the economically productive part of an individual's life over that person's whole life. As with all financial problems, this task is made difficult by time and uncertainty. Merely setting aside a portion of one's income for later use does not mean that it will be there—in real (inflation-adjusted) terms—when it is needed. No investment is riskless if the "run" is long enough. In addition, there is the ordinary risk that the realized return will be lower than the expected return. Finally, no one knows how long he or she is going to live. The need to provide for oneself in old age—when the opportunity to earn labor income is vastly diminished—introduces a kind of uncertainty into life-cycle finance that is not present, or at least not as visible, in institutional investment settings.

The risk that one will outlive one's money is best referred to as "longevity risk." The traditional way that savers have managed this risk is by purchasing life annuities or by having annuitylike cash flow streams purchased for them through defined-benefit (DB) pension plans. (Social Security can also be understood, at least from the viewpoint of the recipient, as an inflation-indexed life annuity.) DB pension plans are declining in importance, however, and a great many workers do not have such a plan. Thus, individual saving and individual investing, including saving and investing through defined-contribution plans, are increasing in importance. For most workers, these efforts provide the only source of retirement income other than Social Security.

It makes sense that annuities would be widely used by workers as a way to replace the guaranteed lifetime income security that once was provided by pensions. But annuities are not as well understood, not as popular, and not as competitively priced, given the increased need for them, as one would hope.

Life insurance is, in a sense, the opposite of an annuity. The purchaser of an annuity bets that he or she will live a long time. The purchaser of life insurance bets that he or she will die soon. Both products have optionlike payoffs, the values of which are conditional on the actual longevity of the purchaser. Life insurance also is seldom used in financial planning, perhaps because, as with annuities, its option value is poorly understood. I do not mean that most people do not have some life insurance—they do. But like annuities, life insurance is not often well integrated into the financial planning process. Why not?

In *Lifetime Financial Advice: Human Capital, Asset Allocation, and Insurance*, four distinguished authors—Roger G. Ibbotson, Moshe A. Milevsky, Peng Chen, CFA, and Kevin X. Zhu—attempt to solve this puzzle. They note that the largest asset that most human beings have, at least when they are young, is their human capital—that is, the present value of their expected future labor income. Human capital interacts with traditional investments, such as stocks, bonds, and real estate, through the correlation structure. But human capital interacts in even more interesting and profitable ways with life insurance and annuities because these assets have payoffs linked to the holder's longevity. The authors of *Lifetime Financial Advice* present a framework for understanding and managing all of these assets holistically.

Ibbotson's earlier work (with numerous co-authors) has documented the past returns of the major asset classes, thus revealing the payoffs received for taking various types of risk, and has presented an approach to forecasting future asset class returns. The asset classes that Ibbotson and his associates are best known for studying are stocks, bonds, bills, and consumer goods (inflation). Knowledge of the past and expected returns of these asset classes, and knowledge of the degree by which realized returns might differ from expected returns, is what makes conventional asset allocation possible. But it is not the whole story. The present monograph finishes the story and makes scientific *financial planning*, which goes beyond conventional asset allocation, possible for individuals by adding in human capital and human capital–contingent assets (life insurance and annuities). With all these arrows in the quiver, an investment adviser can *guarantee* a target standard of living, rather than merely minimize the likelihood of falling below the target, which is all that can be accomplished with conventional asset allocation.

As the Baby Boomers begin to retire, their many trillions of dollars of savings and investments are shifting from accumulation to decumulation, making the ideas and techniques described in *Lifetime Financial Advice* timely and necessary. We hope and expect that researchers will continue to follow this path in the future by placing a much greater emphasis on life-cycle finance than in the past. We intend that upcoming Research Foundation monographs will reflect the heightened emphasis on life-cycle finance. The present monograph is an unusually complete and theoretically sound compendium of knowledge on this topic. We are exceptionally pleased to present it.

Laurence B. Siegel
Research Director
The Research Foundation of CFA Institute

1. Introduction

We can generally categorize a person's life into three financial stages. The first stage is the growing up and getting educated stage. The second stage is the working part of a person's life, and the final stage is retirement. This monograph focuses on the working and the retirement stages of a person's life because these are the two stages when an individual is part of the economy and an investor.

Even though this monograph is not really about the growing up and getting educated stage, this is a critical stage for everyone. The education and skills that we build over this first stage of our lives not only determine who we are but also provide us with a capacity to earn income or wages for the remainder of our lives. This earning power we call "human capital," and we define it as the present value of the anticipated earnings over one's remaining lifetime. The evidence is strong that the amount of education one receives is highly correlated with the present value of earning power. Education can be thought of as an investment in human capital.

One focus of this monograph is on how human capital interacts with financial capital. Understanding this interaction helps us to create, manage, protect, bequest, and especially, appropriately consume our financial resources over our lifetimes. In particular, we propose ways to optimally manage our stock, bond, and so on, asset allocations with various types of insurance products. Along the way, we provide models that potentially enable individuals to customize their financial decision making to their own special circumstances.

On the one hand, as we enter the earning stage of our lives, our human capital is often at its highest point. On the other hand, our financial wealth is usually at a low point. This is the time when we began to convert our human capital into financial capital by earning wages and saving some of these wages. Thus, we call this stage of our lives the "accumulation stage." As our lives progress, we gradually use up the earning power of our human capital, but ideally, we are continually saving some of these earnings and investing them in the financial markets. As our savings continue and we earn returns on our financial investments, our financial capital grows and becomes the dominant part of our total wealth.

As we enter the retirement stage of our lives, our human capital may be almost depleted. It may not be totally gone because we still may have Social Security and defined-benefit pension plans that provide yearly income for the rest of our lives, but our wage-earning power is now very small and does not usually represent the major part of our wealth. Most of us will have little human capital as we enter retirement but substantial financial capital. Over the course of our retirement, we will primarily consume from this financial capital, often bequeathing the remainder to our heirs.

Thus, our total wealth is made up of two parts: our human capital and our financial capital. Recognizing this simple dichotomy dramatically broadens how we analyze financial activities. We desire to create a diversified overall portfolio at the appropriate level of risk. Because human capital is usually relatively low risk (compared with common stocks), we generally want to have a substantial amount of equities in our financial portfolio early in our careers because financial wealth makes up so little of our total wealth (human capital plus financial capital).

Over our lifetimes, our mix of human capital and financial capital changes. In particular, financial capital becomes more dominant as we age so that the lower-risk human capital represents a smaller and smaller piece of the total. As this happens, we will want to be more conservative with our financial capital because it will represent most of our wealth.

Recognizing that human capital is important means that we also want to protect it to the extent we can. Although it is not easy to protect the overall level of our earnings powers, we can financially protect against death, which is the worst-case scenario. Most of us will want to invest in life insurance, which protects us against this mortality risk. Thus, our financial portfolio during the accumulation stage of our lives will typically consist of stocks, bonds, and life insurance.

We face another kind of risk after we retire. During the retirement stage of our lives, we are usually consuming more than our income (i.e., some of our financial capital). Because we cannot perfectly predict how long our retirement will last, there is a danger that we will consume all our financial wealth. The risk of living too long (from a financial point of view) is called "longevity risk." But there is a way to insure against longevity risk, which is to purchase annuity products that pay yearly income as long as one lives. Providing that a person or a couple has sufficient resources to purchase sufficient annuities, they can insure that they will not outlive their wealth.

This monograph is about managing our financial wealth in the context of having both human and financial capital. The portfolio that works best tends to hold stocks and bonds as well as insurance products. We are attempting to put these decisions together in a single framework. Thus, we are trying to provide a theoretical foundation—a framework—and practical solutions for developing investment advice for individual investors throughout their lives.

In this chapter, we review the traditional investment advice model for individual investors, briefly introduce three additional factors that investors need to consider when making investment decisions, and propose a framework for developing lifetime investment advice for individual investors that expands the traditional advice model to include the additional factors that we discuss in the chapter.

The Changing Retirement Landscape

According to the "Survey of Consumer Finances" conducted by the U.S. Federal Reserve Board (2004), the number one reason for individual investors to save and invest is to fund spending in retirement. In other words, funding a comfortable retirement is the primary financial goal for individual investors.

Significant changes in how individual investors finance their retirement spending have occurred in the past 20 years. One major change is the increasing popularity of investment retirement accounts (IRAs) and defined-contribution (DC) plans. Based on data from the Investment Company Institute, retirement assets reached $14.5 trillion in 2005. IRAs and DC plans total roughly half of that amount—which is a tremendous increase from 25 years ago. Today, IRAs and DC plans are replacing traditional defined-benefit (DB) plans as the primary accounts in which to accumulate retirement assets.

Social Security payments and DB pension plans have traditionally provided the bulk of retirement income in the United States. For example, the U.S. Social Security Administration reports that 44 percent of income for people 65 and older came from Social Security income in 2001 and 25 percent came from DB pensions. As **Figure 1.1** shows, according to Employee Benefit Research Institute reports, current retirees (see Panel B) receive almost 70 percent of their retirement income from Social Security and traditional company pension plans whereas today's workers (see Panel A) can expect to have only about one-third of their retirement income funded by these sources (see GAO 2003; EBRI 2000). Increasingly, workers are relying on their DC retirement portfolios and other personal savings as the primary resources for retirement income.

The shift of retirement funding from professionally managed DB plans to personal savings vehicles implies that investors need to make their own decisions about how to allocate retirement savings and what products should be used to generate income in retirement. This shift naturally creates a huge demand for professional investment advice throughout the investor's life cycle (in both the accumulation stage and the retirement stage).

This financial advice must obviously focus on more than simply traditional security selection. Financial advisers will have to familiarize themselves with longevity insurance products and other instruments that provide lifetime income.

In addition, individual investors today face more retirement risk factors than did investors from previous generations. First, the Social Security system and many DB pension plans are at risk, so investors must increasingly rely on their own savings for retirement spending. Second, people today are living longer and could face much higher health-care costs in retirement than members of previous generations. Individual investors increasingly seek professional advice also in dealing with these risk factors.

Figure 1.1. How Will You Pay for Retirement?

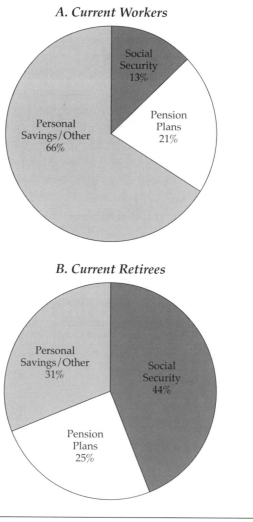

A. Current Workers

Social Security 13%

Pension Plans 21%

Personal Savings/Other 66%

B. Current Retirees

Personal Savings/Other 31%

Social Security 44%

Pension Plans 25%

Source: Based on data from EBRI (2001).

Traditional Advice Model for Individual Investors

The Markowitz (1952) mean–variance framework is widely accepted in academic and practitioner finance as the primary tool for developing asset allocations for individual as well as institutional investors. According to modern portfolio theory, asset allocation is determined by constructing mean–variance-efficient portfolios for various risk levels.[1] Then, based on the investor's risk tolerance, one of these efficient portfolios is selected. Investors follow the asset allocation output to invest their financial assets.

The result of mean–variance analysis is shown in a classic mean–variance diagram. Efficient portfolios are plotted graphically on the *efficient frontier*. Each portfolio on the frontier represents the portfolio with the smallest risk for its level of expected return. The portfolio with the smallest variance is called the "minimum variance" portfolio, and it can be located at the left side of the efficient frontier. These concepts are illustrated in **Figure 1.2**, which uses standard deviation (the square root of variance) for the *x*-axis because the units of standard deviation are easy to interpret.

Figure 1.2.   Mean–Variance-Efficient Frontier

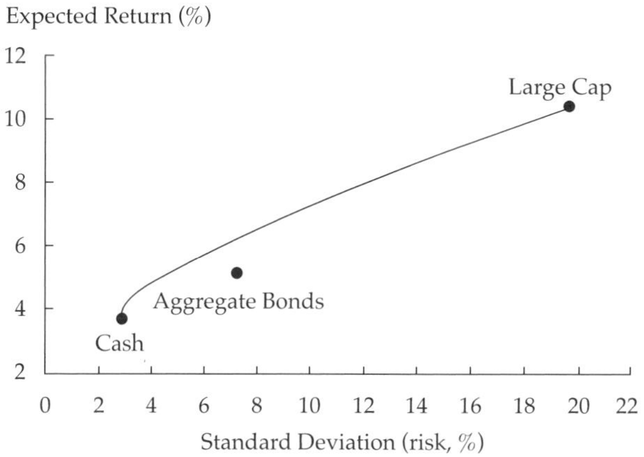

Note: "Large Cap" refers to large-capitalization stocks.

This mean–variance framework emphasizes the importance of taking advantage of the diversification benefits available over time by holding a variety of financial investments or asset classes. When the framework is used to develop investment advice for individual investors, questionnaires are often used to measure the investor's tolerance for risk.

Unfortunately, the framework in **Figure 1.3** considers only the risk–return trade-off in financial assets. It does not consider many other risks that individual investors face throughout their lives.

---

[1]In addition to Markowitz (1952), see Merton (1969, 1971).

Figure 1.3. Traditional Investment Advice Model

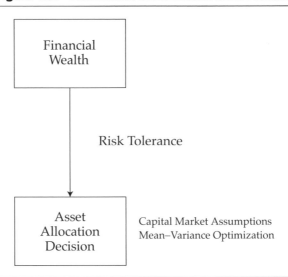

Three Risk Factors and Hedges

We briefly introduce three of the risk factors associated with human capital that investors need to manage—wage earnings risk, mortality risk, and longevity risk—and three types of products that should be considered hedges of those risks. Note that these risk factors, or issues, are often neglected in traditional portfolio analysis. Indeed, one of the main arguments in this monograph is that comprehensive cradle-to-grave financial advice cannot ignore the impact and role of insurance products.

Human Capital, Earnings Risk, and Financial Capital. The traditional mean–variance framework's concentration on diversifying financial assets is a reasonable goal for many institutional investors, but it is not a realistic framework for individual investors who are working and saving for retirement. In fact, this factor is one of the main observations made by Markowitz (1990). From a broad perspective, an investor's total wealth consists of two parts. One is readily tradable financial assets; the other is human capital.

Human capital is defined as the present value of an investor's future labor income. From the economic perspective, labor income can be viewed as a dividend on the investor's human capital. Although human capital is not readily tradable, it is often the single largest asset an investor has. Typically, younger investors have far more human capital than financial capital because young investors have a longer time to work and have had little time to save and accumulate financial wealth. Conversely, older investors tend to have more financial capital than human capital because they have less time to work but have accumulated financial capital over a long career.

One way to reduce wage earnings risk is to save more. This saving converts human capital to financial capital at a higher rate. It also enables the financial capital to have a longer time to grow until retirement. The value of compounding returns in financial capital over time can be very substantial.

And one way to reduce human capital risk is to diversify it with appropriate types of financial capital. Portfolio allocation recommendations that are made without consideration of human capital are not appropriate for many individual investors. To reduce risk, financial assets should be diversified while taking into account human capital assets. For example, the employees of Enron Corporation and WorldCom suffered from extremely poor overall diversification. Their labor income and their financial investments were both in their own companies' stock. When their companies collapsed, both their human capital and their financial capital were heavily affected.

There is growing recognition among academics and practitioners that the risk and return characteristics of human capital—such as wage and salary profiles—should be taken into account when building portfolios for individual investors. Well-known financial scholars and commentators have pointed out the importance of including the magnitude of human capital, its volatility, and its correlation with other assets into a personal risk management perspective.[2] Yet, Benartzi (2001) showed that many investors invest heavily in the stock of the company they work for. He found for 1993 that roughly a third of plan assets were invested in company stock. Benartzi argued that such investment is not efficient because company stock is not only an undiversified risky investment; it is also highly correlated with the person's human capital.[3]

Appropriate investment advice for individual investors is to invest financial wealth in an asset that is not highly correlated with their human capital in order to maximize diversification benefits over the entire portfolio. For people with "safe" human capital, it may be appropriate to invest their financial assets aggressively.

Mortality Risk and Life Insurance. Because human capital is often the biggest asset an investor has, protecting human capital from potential risks should also be part of overall investment advice. A unique risk aspect of an investor's human capital is mortality risk—the loss of human capital to the household in the unfortunate event of premature death of the worker. This loss of human capital can have a devastating impact on the financial well-being of a family.

Life insurance has long been used to hedge against mortality risk. Typically, the greater the value of human capital, the more life insurance the family demands. Intuitively, human capital affects not only optimal life insurance demand but also

---

[2]For example, Bodie, Merton, and Samuelson (1992); Campbell and Viceira (2002); Merton (2003).
[3]Meulbroek (2002) estimated that a large position in company stock held over a long period is effectively, after accounting for the costs of inadequate diversification, worth less than 50 cents on the dollar.

optimal asset allocation. But these two important financial decisions—the demand for life insurance and optimal asset allocation—have, however, consistently been analyzed *separately* in theory and practice. We have found few references in either the risk/insurance literature or the investment/finance literature to the importance of considering these decisions jointly within the context of a life-cycle model of consumption and investment. Popular investment and financial planning advice regarding how much life insurance one should carry is seldom framed in terms of the riskiness of one's human capital. And optimal asset allocation is only lately being framed in terms of the risk characteristics of human capital, and rarely is it integrated with life insurance decisions.

Fortunately, in the event of death, life insurance can be a perfect hedge for human capital. That is, term life insurance and human capital have a negative 100 percent correlation with each other in the "living" versus "dead" states; if one pays off at the end of the year, the other does not, and vice versa. Thus, the combination of the two provides diversification to an investor's total portfolio. The many reasons for considering these decisions and products jointly become even more powerful once investors approach and enter their retirement years.

Longevity Risk and the Lifetime-Payout Annuity. The shift in retirement funding from professionally managed DB plans to DC personal savings vehicles implies that investors need to make their own decisions not only about how to allocate retirement savings but also about what products should be used to generate income throughout retirement. Investors must consider two important risk factors when making these decisions. One is financial market risk (i.e., volatility in the capital markets that causes portfolio values to fluctuate). If the market drops or corrections occur early during retirement, the portfolio may not be able to weather the added stress of systematic consumption withdrawals. The portfolio may then be unable to provide the necessary income for the person's desired lifestyle. The second important risk factor is longevity risk—that is, the risk of outliving the portfolio. Life expectancies have been increasing, and retirees should be aware of their substantial chance of a long retirement and plan accordingly. This risk is faced by every investor but especially those taking advantage of early retirement offers or those who have a family history of longevity.

Increasingly, all retirees will need to balance income and expenditures over a longer period of time than in the past. One factor that is increasing the average length of time spent in retirement is a long-term trend toward early retirement. For example, in the United States, nearly half of all men now leave the workforce by age 62 and almost half of all women are out of the workforce by age 60. A second factor is that this decline in the average retirement age has occurred in an environment of rising life expectancies for retirees. Since 1940, falling mortality rates have added almost 4 years to the expected life span of a 65-year-old male and more than 5 years to the life expectancy of a 65-year-old female.

Figure 1.4 illustrates the survival probability of a 65-year-old. The first bar of each pair shows the probability of at least one person from a married couple surviving to various ages, and the second bar shows the probability of an individual surviving to various ages. For married couples, in more than 80 percent of the cases, at least one spouse will probably still be alive at age 85.

Figure 1.4. Probability of Living to 100

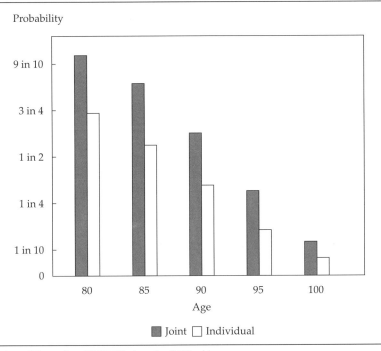

Source: Society of Actuaries, 1996 U.S. Annuity 2000 table.

Longevity is increasing not simply in the United Sates but also around the world. Longevity risk, like mortality risk, is independent of financial market risk. Unlike mortality risk, longevity risk is borne by the investor directly. Also unlike mortality risk, longevity risk is related to income needs and so, logically, should be directly related to asset allocation.

A number of recent articles—for example, Ameriks, Veres, and Warshawsky (2001); Bengen (2001); Milevsky and Robinson (2005); Milevsky, Moore, and Young (2006)—have focused financial professionals' as well as academics' attention on longevity risk in retirement. A growing body of literature is trying to use traditional portfolio management and investment technology to model personal insurance and pension decisions. But simple retirement planning approaches ignore longevity risk by assuming that an investor need only plan to age 85. It is true that 85 is roughly the life expectancy for a 65-year-old individual, but life *expectancy* is only a measure of central tendency or a halfway point estimate. Almost by definition, half of all investors will exceed their life expectancy. And for a married couple, the odds are more than 80 percent that at least one spouse will live beyond this milestone. If investors use an 85-year life expectancy to plan their retirement income needs, many of them will use up their retirement resources (other than government and corporate pensions) long before actual mortality. This longevity risk—the risk of outliving one's resources—is substantial and is the reason that lifetime annuities (payout annuities) should also be an integral part of many retirement plans.

A lifetime-payout annuity is an insurance product that converts an accumulated investment into income that the insurance company pays out over the life of the investor.[4] Payout annuities are the opposite of life insurance. Consumers buy life insurance because they are afraid of dying too soon and leaving family and loved ones in financial need. They buy payout annuities because they are concerned about living too long and running out of assets during their lifetime.

Insurance companies can afford to provide this lifelong benefit by (1) spreading the longevity risk over a large group of annuitants and (2) making careful and conservative assumptions about the rate of return they will earn on their assets. Spreading or pooling the longevity risk means that individuals who do not reach their life expectancy, as calculated by actuarial mortality tables, subsidize those who exceed it. Investors who buy lifetime-payout annuities pool their portfolios together and collectively ensure that everybody will receive payments as long as each lives. Because of the unique longevity insurance features embedded in lifetime-payout annuities, they can play a significant role in many investors' retirement portfolios.

An Integrated Framework

This monograph was inspired by the need to expand the traditional investment advice framework shown in Figure 1.3 to integrate the special risk factors of individual investors into their investment decisions. The main objective of our study was to review the existing literature and develop original solutions—specifically:

1. To analyze the asset allocation decisions of individual investors while taking into consideration human capital characteristics—namely, the size of human capital, its volatility, and its correlation with other assets.

---

[4]In this monograph, we use various terms synonymously to represent *lifetime-payout annuity*—lifetime annuity, payout annuity, and immediate annuity.

2. To analyze jointly the decision as to how much life insurance a family unit should have to protect against the loss of its breadwinner and how the family should allocate its financial resources between risk-free (bondlike) and risky (stocklike) assets within the dynamics of labor income and human capital.[5]

3. To analyze the transition from the accumulation (saving) phase to the distribution (spending) phase of retirement planning within the context of a life-cycle model that emphasizes the role of payout annuities and longevity insurance because of the continuing erosion of traditional DB pensions.

To summarize, the purpose here is to parsimoniously merge the factors of human capital, investment allocation, life insurance, and longevity insurance into a conventional framework of portfolio choice and asset allocation. We plan to establish a unified framework to study the total asset allocation decision in accumulation and retirement, which includes both financial market risk as well as other risk factors. We will try to achieve this goal with a minimal amount of technical modeling and, instead, emphasize intuition and examples, perhaps at the expense of some rigor. In some cases, we will provide the reader with references to more advanced material or material that delves into the mathematics of an idea. Furthermore, we provide some of the technical material in appendices to some of the chapters.

We are specifically interested in the interaction between the demand for life insurance, payout annuities, and asset allocation when the correlation between the investor's labor income process and financial market returns is not zero. This project significantly expands our earlier works on similar topics.[6] First, we analyze portfolio choice decisions at both the preretirement stage and in retirement, thus presenting a complete life-cycle picture. Second, instead of focusing on traditional utility models, we explore lifetime objective functions and various computational techniques when solving the problem. Third, we include a comprehensive literature review that provides the reader with background information on previous contributions to the field.

The rest of the monograph is organized into two general segments. This first segment, which includes Chapters 2 and 3, investigates the advice framework in the accumulation stage. Chapter 2 analyzes the impact of human capital on the asset allocation decision. Chapter 3 presents the combined framework that includes both

---

[5]How much an investor should consume or save is another important decision that is frequently tied to the concept of human capital. In this monograph, we focus on only the asset allocation and life insurance decisions; therefore, our model has been simplified by the assumption that the investor has already decided how much to consume or save. Our numerical cases assume that the investor saves a constant 10 percent of salary each year.

[6]For example, Chen and Milevsky (2003); Huang, Milevsky, and Wang (2005); Chen, Ibbotson, Milevsky, and Zhu (2006).

the asset allocation decision and the life insurance decision. We present a number of case studies to illustrate the interaction between the two decisions and the effects of various factors.

The second segment, which includes Chapters 4, 5, and 6, investigates the retirement stage. In Chapter 4, we analyze the risk factors that investors face in retirement. We focus our discussion on longevity risk and the potential role that lifetime-payout annuities can play in managing longevity risk. In Chapter 5, we present the model for constructing optimal asset allocations that include lifetime-payout annuities for retirement portfolios.[7] In Chapter 6, we discuss the timing of the annuitization decision (i.e., when investors should annuitize their assets).

Chapter 7 provides an overall summary of the framework and recommendations from the accumulation stage through the retirement stage and discusses implications of our work.

---

[7]We believe we are the first to analyze longevity risk in the broader asset allocation framework and develop the optimal allocation to payout annuities. Ibbotson Associates has been granted a patent on developing optimal allocations that include traditional assets and payout annuities (patent number 7120601).

2. Human Capital and Asset Allocation Advice

In determinations of the appropriate asset allocation for individual investors, the level of risk a person can afford or tolerate depends not only on the individual's psychological attitude toward risk but also on his or her total financial situation (including the types and sources of income). Earning ability outside of investments is important in determining capacity for risk. People with high earning ability are able to take more risk because they can easily recoup financial losses.[8] In his well-known *A Random Walk Down Wall Street*, Malkiel (2004) stated, "The risks you can afford to take depend on your total financial situation, including the types and sources of your income exclusive of investment income" (p. 342). A person's financial situation and earning ability can often be captured by taking the person's human capital into consideration.

A fundamental element in financial planning advice is that younger investors (or investors with longer investment horizons) should invest aggressively. This advice is a direct application of the human capital concept. The impact of human capital on an investor's optimal asset allocation has been studied by many academic researchers. And many financial planners, following the principles of the human capital concept, automatically adjust the risk levels of an individual investor's portfolio over the investor's life stages. In this chapter, we discuss why incorporating human capital into an investor's asset allocation decision is important. We first introduce the concept of human capital; then, we describe the importance of human capital in determining asset allocation. Finally, we use case studies to illustrate this role of human capital.

What Is Human Capital?

An investor's total wealth consists of two parts. One is readily tradable financial assets, such as the assets in a 401(k) plan, individual retirement account, or mutual fund; the other is human capital. Human capital is defined as the economic present value of an investor's future labor income. Economic theory predicts that investors make asset allocation decisions to maximize their lifetime utilities through consumption. These decisions are closely linked to human capital.

---

[8]Educational attainments and work experience are the two most significant factors determining a person's earning ability.

Although human capital is not readily tradable, it is often the single largest asset an investor has. Typically, younger investors have far more human capital than financial capital because they have many years to work and they have had few years to save and accumulate financial wealth. Conversely, older investors tend to have more financial capital than human capital because they have fewer years ahead to work but have accumulated financial capital. *Human capital should be treated like any other asset class*; it has its own risk and return properties and its own correlations with other financial asset classes.

Role of Human Capital in Asset Allocation

In investing for long-term goals, the allocation of asset categories in the portfolio is one of the most crucial decisions (Ibbotson and Kaplan 2000). However, many asset allocation advisers focus on only the risk–return characteristics of readily tradable financial assets. These advisers ignore human capital, which is often the single largest asset an investor has in his or her personal balance sheet. If asset allocation is indeed a critical determinant of investment and financial success, then given the large magnitude of human capital, one must include it.

Intuitive Examples of Portfolio Diversification Involving Human Capital. Investors should make sure that their total (i.e., human capital plus financial capital) portfolios are properly diversified. In simple words, investment advisers need to incorporate assets in such a way that when one type of capital zigs, the other zags. Therefore, in the early stages of the life cycle, financial and investment capital should be used to hedge and diversify human capital rather than used naively to build wealth. Think of financial investable assets as a defense and protection against adverse shocks to human capital (i.e., salaries and wages), not an isolated pot of money to be blindly allocated for the long run.

For example, for a tenured university professor of finance, human capital—and the subsequent pension to which the professor is entitled—has the properties of a fixed-income bond fund that entitles the professor to monthly coupons. The professor's human capital is similar to an inflation-adjusted, real-return bond. In light of the risk and return characteristics of this human capital, therefore, the professor has little need for fixed-income bonds, money market funds, or even Treasury Inflation-Protected Securities (real-return bonds) in his financial portfolio. By placing the investment money elsewhere, the total portfolio of human and financial capital will be well balanced despite the fact that if each is viewed in isolation, the financial capital and human capital are not diversified.

In contrast to this professor, many *students* of finance might expect to earn a lot more than their university professor during their lifetimes, but their relative incomes and bonuses will fluctuate from year to year in relation to the performance of the stock market, the industry they work in, and the unpredictable vagaries of their labor market. Their human capital will be almost entirely invested in equity, so early in their working careers, their financial capital should be tilted slightly more toward bonds and other fixed-income products. Of course, when they are young and can tolerate the ups and downs in the market, they should have some exposure to equities. But all else being equal, two individuals who are exactly 35 years old and have exactly the same projected annual income and retirement horizon should not have the same equity portfolio structure if their human capital differs in risk characteristics. Certainly, simplistic rules like "100 minus age should be invested in equities" have no room in a sophisticated, holistic framework of wealth management.

It may seem odd to advise future practitioners in the equity industry *not* to "put their money where their mouths are" (i.e., not to invest more aggressively in the stock market), but in fact, hedging human capital risks is prudent risk management. Indeed, perhaps with some tongue in cheek, we might disagree with famed investor and stock market guru Peter Lynch and argue that you should *not* invest in things you are familiar with but, rather, in industries and companies you know nothing or little about. Those investments will have little correlation with your human capital. Remember the engineers, technicians, and computer scientists who thought they knew the high-technology industry and whose human capital was invested in the same industry; they learned the importance of the human capital concept the hard way.

Portfolio allocation recommendations that do not consider the individual's human capital are not appropriate for many individual investors who are working and saving for retirement.

Academic Literature. In the late 1960s, economists developed models that implied that individuals should optimally maintain constant portfolio weights throughout their lives (Samuelson 1969, Merton 1969). An important assumption of these models was that investors have no labor income (or human capital). This assumption is not realistic, however, as we have discussed, because most investors do have labor income. If labor income is included in the portfolio choice model, individuals will optimally change their allocations of financial assets in a pattern related to the life cycle. In other words, the optimal asset allocation depends on the risk–return characteristics of their labor income and the flexibility of their labor income (such as how much or how long the investor works).

Bodie, Merton, and Samuelson (1992) studied the impact of labor income flexibility on investment strategy. They found that investors with a high degree of labor flexibility should take more risk in their investment portfolios. For example, younger investors may invest more of their financial assets in risky assets than older investors because the young have more flexibility in their working lives.

Hanna and Chen (1997) explored optimal asset allocation by using a simulation method that considered human capital and various investment horizons. Assuming human capital is a risk-free asset, they found that for most investors with long horizons, an all-equity portfolio is optimal.

In our modeling framework, which we will present in a moment, investors adjust their financial portfolios to compensate for their risk exposure to nontradable human capital.[9] The key theoretical implications are as follows: (1) younger investors invest more in stocks than older investors; (2) investors with safe labor income (thus safe human capital) invest more of their financial portfolio in stocks; (3) investors with labor income that is highly correlated with the stock markets invest their financial assets in less risky assets; and (4) the ability to adjust labor supply (i.e., higher flexibility) increases an investor's allocation to stocks.

Empirical studies show, however, that most investors do not efficiently diversify their financial portfolios in light of the risk of their human capital. Benartzi (2001) and Benartzi and Thaler (2001) showed that many investors use primitive methods to determine their asset allocations and many of them invest heavily in the stock of the company for which they work.[10] Davis and Willen (2000) estimated the correlation between labor income and equity market returns by using the U.S. Department of Labor's "Current Occupation Survey." They found that human capital has a low correlation (−0.2 to 0.1) with aggregate equity markets. The implication is that the typical investor need not worry about his or her human capital being highly correlated with the stock market when making asset allocation decisions; thus, most investors can invest the majority of their financial wealth in risky assets.[11]

Empirical studies have also found that for the majority of U.S. households, human capital is the dominant asset. Using the U.S. Federal Reserve Board's 1992 "Survey of Consumer Finances," Lee and Hanna (1995) estimated that the ratio of financial assets to total wealth (including human capital) was 1.3 percent for the median household. Thus, for half of the households, financial assets represented less than 1.3 percent of total wealth. The 75th percentile of this ratio was 5.7 percent. The 90th percentile was 17.4 percent. In short, financial assets represented a high percentage of total wealth for only a small proportion of U.S. households. The small magnitude of these numbers places a significant burden on financial advisers to learn more about their clients' human capital, which is such a valuable component of personal balance sheets.

---

[9]See Merton (1971); Bodie, Merton, and Samuelson (1992); Heaton and Lucas (1997); Jagannathan and Kocherlakota (1996); Campbell and Viceira (2002).

[10]Heaton and Lucas (2000) showed that wealthy households with high and variable business income invest less in the stock market than similarly wealthy households without that sort of business income, which is consistent with the theoretical prediction.

[11]Although this might be true in aggregate, it can vary widely among individuals.

Figure 2.1 shows the relationships among financial capital, human capital, other factors (such as savings and the investor's aversion to risk), and the asset allocation of financial capital.

Figure 2.1. Human Capital and Asset Allocation

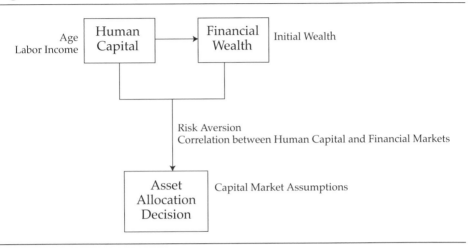

Human Capital and Asset Allocation Modeling.
This section provides a general overview of how to determine optimal asset allocation while considering human capital. Appendix A contains a detailed specification of the model, which is the basis of our numerical examples and case studies.

Human capital can be calculated from the following equation:

$$HC(x) = \sum_{t=x+1}^{n} \frac{E[h_t]}{(1+r+v)^{t-x}}, \tag{2.1}$$

where

x	= current age
$HC(x)$	= human capital at age x
h_t	= earnings for year t adjusted for inflation before retirement and after retirement, adjusted for Social Security and pension payments
n	= life expectancy
r	= inflation-adjusted risk-free rate
v	= discount rate[12]

---

[12]The discount rate should be adjusted to the risk level of the person's labor income (see Appendix A).

In the model, we assume there are two asset classes.[13] The investor can allocate financial wealth between a risk-free asset and a risky asset (i.e., bonds and stocks). We assume the investor has financial capital W_t at the beginning of period t. The investor chooses the optimal allocation involving the risk-free asset and the risky asset that will maximize expected utility of total wealth, which is the sum of financial capital and human capital, $W_{t+1} + H_{t+1}$. We assume the investor follows the constant relative risk aversion (CRRA) utility function. In our case, it is

$$U = \frac{\left(W_{t+1} + H_{t+1}\right)^{1-\gamma}}{1-\gamma} \tag{2.2}$$

for $\gamma \neq 1$ and

$$U = \ln\left(W_{t+1} + H_{t+1}\right) \tag{2.3}$$

for $\gamma = 1$. In Equations 2.2 and 2.3, γ is the coefficient of relative risk aversion and is greater than zero.

In the model, labor income and the return of risky assets are correlated. The optimization problem the investor faces is expressed in detail in Appendix A.

The investor's human capital can be viewed as a "stock" if both the correlation with a given financial market index and the volatility of labor income are high. It can be viewed as a "bond" if both correlation and volatility are low. In between these two extremes, human capital is a diversified portfolio of stocks and bonds, plus idiosyncratic risk.[14] We are quite cognizant of the difficulties involved in calibrating these variables that were pointed out by Davis and Willen (2000), and we rely on some of their parameters for our numerical examples in the following case studies.

Case Studies

In the cases, we look at some specific parameters and the resulting optimal portfolios. In the first case, we treat future labor income as certain (i.e., there is no uncertainty in the labor income). The model indicates that human capital in this case is a risk-free asset (as in the case of our professor). Then, we add uncertainty into consideration. Specifically, we treat human capital as a risky asset.

---

[13]The model was inspired by an early model by Campbell (1980) that seeks to maximize the total wealth of an investor in a one-period framework. The total wealth consists of the investor's financial wealth and human capital. In this chapter, we focus on the asset allocation decision for investors' financial capital instead of the life insurance decision in Campbell's paper.

[14]Note that when we make statements such as "this person's human capital is 40 percent long-term bonds, 30 percent financial services, and 30 percent utilities," we mean that the unpredictable shocks to future wages have a given correlation structure with the named subindices. Thus, as in our previous example, the tenured university professor could be considered to be a 100 percent real-return (inflation-indexed) bond because no shocks to his wages would be linked to any financial subindex.

For example, let us assume that we have a male U.S. investor whose annual income is expected to grow with inflation and there is no uncertainty about his annual income—which is $50,000. He saves 10 percent of his income each year. He expects to receive Social Security payments of $10,000 each year (in today's dollars) when he retires at age 65. His current financial wealth is $50,000, of which 40 percent is invested in a risk-free asset and 60 percent is invested in a risky asset. Finally, he rebalances his financial portfolio annually back to the initial portfolio allocation. Human capital was estimated by using Equation 2.1.

Financial capital for the examples, in contrast to human capital, can be easily parameterized on the basis of the evolution of returns over time. Table 2.1 provides the capital market assumptions that are used in this computation for this and other cases in this chapter and Chapter 3.

Table 2.1. Capital Market Return Assumptions

Asset	Compounded Annual Return	Risk (standard deviation)
Risk free (bonds)	5%	—
Risky (stocks)	9	20%
Inflation	3	—

Note: These capital market assumptions are comparable to the historical performance of U.S. stocks and bonds from 1926 to 2006, after adjusting for investment expenses the investor would have to pay. According to Ibbotson Associates (2006), the compounded annual return for that period was 10.36 percent for the S&P 500 Index (with a standard deviation of 20.2 percent), 5.47 percent for U.S. government bonds, and 3.04 percent for inflation.

Figures 2.2 and 2.3 illustrate the relationships of financial capital, human capital, and total wealth (defined as the sum of financial capital and human capital) that investors might expect over their working (preretirement) years from age 25 to age 65. For example, under our assumptions and calculation of human capital, for a male investor who is 25 years old, Figure 2.2 shows that his human capital is estimated to be about $800,000; Figure 2.3 shows that it represents 94 percent of his total wealth and far outweighs his financial capital at that age. His financial capital is only $50,000. As the investor gets older and continues to make savings contributions, these monies plus the return from the existing portfolio increase the proportion of financial capital. At age 65, Figure 2.2 shows the human capital decreasing to $128,000 (to come from future Social Security payments) and the financial portfolio peaking just above $1.2 million.

Figure 2.2. Expected Financial Capital, Human Capital, and Total Wealth over Life Cycle with Optimal Asset Allocation

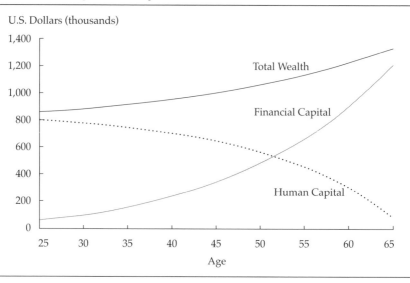

Figure 2.3. Financial Capital and Human Capital as Share of Total Wealth over Life Cycle

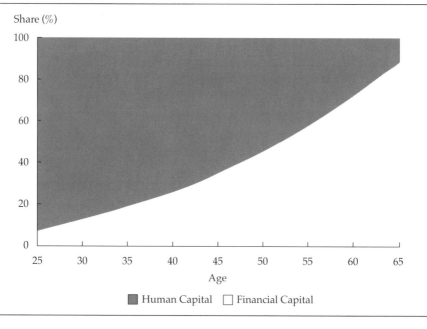

Case #1. Human Capital as a Risk-Free Asset. In this case, we assume that there is no uncertainty about the investor's annual income, so his human capital is a risk-free asset because it is the present value of future income. He is age 25 with annual income of $50,000 and current financial wealth of $50,000. The coefficient of relative risk aversion for this investor is assumed to be 5.5 (i.e., $\gamma = 5.5$).

Figure 2.4 shows the optimal asset allocation of this investor's financial capital from age 25 to 65. As can be seen, the allocation of financial wealth to risk-free assets increases over time. In other words, the investor increases allocations to the risk-free asset in order to maintain a desired risk exposure in the total wealth portfolio. Households will tend to hold proportionately less of the risk-free financial asset when young (when the value of human capital is large) and tend to increase the proportion of financial wealth held in the risk-free financial asset as they age (as the amount of human capital declines).

Figure 2.4. Case #1: Optimal Asset Allocation to the Risk-Free Asset over Life Cycle

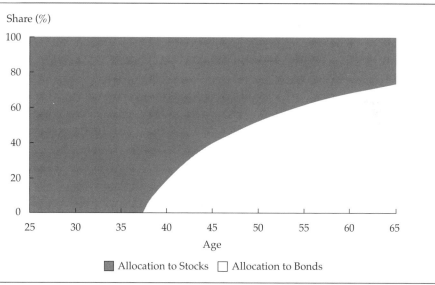

Note: Risk tolerance level at 5.5.

Now, let's analyze the risk exposure of the investor's total portfolio at different ages in this case. When considering human capital, to keep the desired risk exposure of his total portfolio at the level indicated by $\gamma = 5.5$, the investor will choose a 100 percent stock asset allocation because he already has 94 percent of his total wealth (represented by his human capital) invested in bonds. Investing 100 percent in stocks is the closest we can get his total portfolio to the target desired risk exposure level without borrowing. When the investor is 45, his total wealth consists of about 40 percent financial assets and 60 percent human capital; the asset allocation for his financial assets is about 60 percent stocks and 40 percent bonds. At age 65, he ends up with a financial portfolio of 27 percent stock and 73 percent bonds.

This simple example illustrates that when an investor's human capital is riskless, the investor should invest more in stocks than an investor closer to retirement, and when an investor gets older, his or her human capital will decrease and financial capital will increase. Thus, the investor should gradually scale back the amount invested in stocks.

Unfortunately, although investors are almost always given the discretion to change their allocations to various assets and account managers usually even maintain a website for this purpose, empirical studies (e.g., Ameriks and Zeldes 2001) suggest that only a small minority of investors actually make any adjustments.

Case #2. Human Capital as a Risky Asset. In Case #1, we assumed that human capital was 100 percent risk free. But only a small portion of investors would have this kind of "safe" human capital. Labor income is uncertain for most investors for a number of reasons, including the possibilities of losing one's job or being laid off. The uncertainty in labor income makes human capital a risky asset.

But the riskiness varies by individual; for example, a business owner, a stock portfolio manager, a stockbroker, and a schoolteacher have different risk profiles in their human capital. To incorporate human capital in total wealth, we need to consider the unique risk and return characteristics of each individual's human capital.

There are two basic types of risk for an investor's human capital. The first type can be treated as risk related to other risky assets (such as stocks). The second type is risk uncorrelated with the stock market. Let's look at the two types and how they affect optimal asset allocation.

To analyze the impact of the two types of human capital risk on the investor's allocation of financial capital, we constructed the following two scenarios. In Scenario 1, human capital is risky and highly correlated with the stock market (α_h = 0.2, where α_h is the volatility of the shocks to the labor income, and ρ_{hs} = 0.5, where ρ_{hs} is the correlation between shocks to labor income and shocks to the risky asset's returns). In Scenario 2, human capital is risky but it is uncorrelated with the stock market (α_h = 0.2 and ρ_{hs} = 0).

Figure 2.5 shows the optimal asset allocations of financial capital in the two scenarios. The assumptions used in Case 1 prevail except for the assumption about volatility and correlation between human capital and the stock market.

Let's start by analyzing the first type of risk (Scenario 1), in which the human capital risk is highly correlated with the risk of other risky financial assets. A simple example of this scenario would be the perfect correlation of labor income with the

Figure 2.5. Case #2: Proportion of Risk-Free Asset in Scenarios 1 and 2

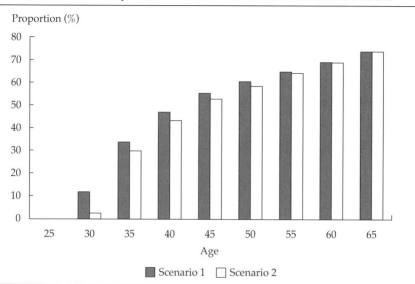

payoffs from holding the aggregate stock market—for example, a stockbroker or a stock portfolio manager. In this situation, our hypothetical investor will use his financial assets to balance his human capital risk. The stockbroker's human capital is far more sensitive to the stock market than a schoolteacher's. If a stockbroker and a schoolteacher have the same total wealth and similar risk tolerances, human capital theory recommends that the stockbroker invest a smaller portion of his financial assets in the stock market than the schoolteacher because the stockbroker has implicitly invested his human capital in the stock market. For young investors with equitylike human capital, the financial assets should be invested predominantly in fixed-income assets. Because the value of one's human capital declines with age, the share of risk-free assets in the stockbroker's portfolio will also decline and the share of risky assets in the portfolio of financial assets will rise until retirement.

Now, let's consider Scenario 2, in which the investor's labor income is risky but not correlated with the payoffs of the risky assets (i.e., is independent of financial market risk). In this case, the investor's optimal financial asset allocation follows, by and large, the same pattern as the case in which the investor's human capital is risk free—especially when the risk of human capital is small (variance in the income over time is small). The reason is that, similar to the risk-free asset, human capital is uncorrelated with financial market risk. When the risk of human capital increases, however, the investor should reduce overall risk in the financial portfolio. In other words, if your occupational income (and future prospects for income) is uncertain, you should refrain from taking too much risk with your financial capital.

Case #3. Impact of Initial Financial Wealth. The purpose of this case is to show the impact of different amounts of current financial wealth on optimal asset allocation. Assume that we hold the investor's age at 45 and set risk preference at a moderate level (a CRRA risk-aversion coefficient of 4). The correlation between shocks to labor income and risky-asset returns is 0.2, and the volatility of shocks to labor income is 5 percent. The optimal allocations to the risk-free asset for various levels of initial financial wealth are presented in **Figure 2.6**.

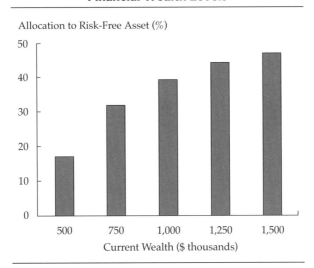

Figure 2.6. Case #3: Optimal Asset Allocation to the Risk-Free Asset at Various Financial Wealth Levels

Figure 2.6 shows that the optimal allocation to the risk-free asset increases with initial wealth. This situation may seem to be inconsistent with the CRRA utility function because the CRRA utility function implies that the optimal asset allocation will not change with the amount of wealth the investor has. Note, however, that "wealth" here includes both financial wealth and human capital. In fact, this situation is a classic example of the impact of human capital on optimal asset allocation. An increase in initial financial wealth not only increases total wealth but also reduces the percentage of total wealth represented by human capital. In this case, human capital is less risky than the risky asset.[15] When initial wealth is low, human capital dominates total wealth and asset allocation. As a result, to achieve the target asset allocation of a moderate investor—say, an allocation of 60 percent

---

[15]In this case, income has a real growth rate of 0 percent and a standard deviation of 5 percent, yet the expected real return on stocks is 8 percent and the standard deviation for stock returns is 20 percent.

to the risk-free asset and 40 percent to the risky asset—the closest allocation is to invest 100 percent of financial wealth in the risky asset because human capital is illiquid. As initial wealth rises, the asset allocation gradually approaches the target asset allocation that a moderately risk-averse investor desires.

In summary, for a typical investor whose human capital is less risky than the stock market, the optimal asset allocation is more conservative the more financial assets the investor has.

Case #4. Correlation between Wage Growth Rate and Stock Returns. In this case, we examine the impact of the correlation between shocks to labor income and shocks to the risky asset's returns. In particular, we want to evaluate asset allocation decisions for investors with human capital that is highly correlated with stocks. Examples are an investor's income that is closely linked to the stock performance of her employer's company or an investor's compensation that is highly influenced by the financial markets (e.g., the investor works in the financial industry).

Again, the investor's age is 45 and the coefficient of relative risk aversion is 4. The amount of financial capital is $500,000. The optimal asset allocations to the risk-free asset for various correlations are presented in **Figure 2.7**.

Figure 2.7.   Case #4: Optimal Asset Allocation to the Risk-Free Asset at Various Correlation Levels

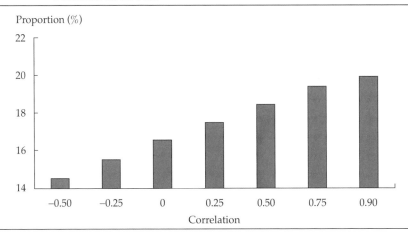

As Figure 2.7 shows, the optimal allocation becomes more conservative (i.e., more assets are allocated to the risk-free asset), with increasing correlation between income and stock market returns. One way to look at this outcome is that a higher correlation between human capital and the stock market results in less diversification and thus higher risk for the total portfolio (human capital plus financial capital).

To reduce this risk, an investor must invest more financial wealth in the risk-free asset. Another way to look at this result is in terms of *certainty equivalents* (or utility equivalents) of wealth. The higher the uncertainty (or volatility), all else being equal, the lower the certainty-equivalent value. In utility terms, with increasing correlation and rising volatility, this investor is actually poorer!

Implications for Advisers. A financial adviser or consultant should be aware of the following issues when developing a long-term asset allocation plan for typical individual investors:

1. Investors should invest financial assets in such a way as to diversify and balance out their human capital.

2. A young investor with relatively safe human capital assets and greater flexibility of labor supply should invest more financial assets in risky assets, such as stocks, than an older investor should, perhaps even with leverage and debt. The portion of financial assets allocated to stocks should be reduced as the investor gets older. Also, if the stock market performs well, the investor's financial capital will grow, and again, the implication is to reduce the portion of financial assets invested in stocks.

3. An investor with human capital that has a high correlation with stock market risk should also reduce the allocation to risky assets in the financial portfolio and increase the allocation to assets that are less correlated with the stock market.[16]

In short, the risk characteristics of human capital have a significant impact on optimal financial portfolio allocation. Therefore, to effectively incorporate human capital into making the asset allocation decision, financial advisers and consultants need to determine (1) whether the investor's human capital is risk free or risky and (2) whether the risk is highly correlated with financial market risk.

Summary

Human capital is defined as the present value of future labor income. Human capital—not financial assets—is usually the dominant asset for young and middle-aged people.

Many academic researchers have advocated considering human capital when developing portfolio allocations of an investor's financial assets. That is, investors should invest their financial assets in such a way as to diversify and balance their human capital.

In addition to the size of the investor's human capital, its risk–return characteristics, its relationship to other financial assets, and the flexibility of the investor's labor supply also have significant effects on how an investor should allocate financial

---

[16]For example, all else being equal, alternative assets with low correlations with the stock market (e.g., commodities, certain hedge funds) can be attractive for these investors.

assets. In general, a typical young investor would be well advised to hold an all-stock investment portfolio (perhaps even with leverage) because the investor can easily offset any disastrous returns in the short run by adjusting his or her future investment strategy, labor supply, consumption, and/or savings. As the investor becomes older, the proportion of human capital in total wealth becomes smaller; therefore, the financial portfolio should become less aggressive.

Although the typical U.S. investor's income is unlikely to be highly correlated with the aggregate stock market (based on results reported by Davis and Willen 2000), many investors' incomes may be highly correlated with a specific company's market experience. Company executives, stockbrokers, and stock portfolio managers (whose labor income and human capital are highly correlated with risky assets) should have financial portfolios invested in assets that are little correlated with the stock market (e.g., bonds).

3. Human Capital, Life Insurance, and Asset Allocation

In the previous chapter, we discussed how human capital plays an important role in developing the appropriate investment recommendations for individual investors. In addition, recognition is growing among academics and practitioners that the risk and return characteristics of human capital (wage and salary profiles) should be taken into account when building portfolios for the individual investor. Therefore, we expanded the traditional investment advice framework to include not only an investor's financial capital but also human capital. To illustrate the effect of human capital in the expanded framework, we used case studies in which the human capital characteristics were quite different.

In this chapter, we study another (perhaps even more important) risk aspect of human capital—*mortality risk*.[17] And we further expand the framework developed in Chapter 2 to include the life insurance decision. We first explain the rationale for examining the life insurance decision together with the asset allocation decision. We develop a unified model to provide practical guidelines on developing optimal asset allocation and life insurance allocation for individual investors in their preretirement years (accumulation stage). We also provide a number of case studies in which we illustrate model allocations that depend on income, age, and tolerance for financial risk.

Life Insurance and Asset Allocation Decisions

A unique aspect of an investor's human capital is mortality risk—the family's loss of human capital in the unfortunate event of the investor's premature death. This risk is huge for many individual investors because human capital is their dominant asset.

Life insurance has long been used to hedge against mortality risk. Typically, the greater the value of the human capital, the more life insurance the family demands. Intuitively, human capital affects not only optimal asset allocation but also optimal life insurance demand. These two important financial decisions have consistently been analyzed separately, however, in theory and practice. We found few references in the literature to the need to consider these decisions jointly and within the context of a life-cycle model of consumption and investment. Popular investment and financial planning advice regarding how much life insurance one should acquire is never framed in terms of the riskiness of one's human capital. And

---

[17]Chapter 3 is partly based on material in Chen, Ibbotson, Milevsky, and Zhu (2006).

©2007, The Research Foundation of CFA Institute

the optimal asset allocation decision has only lately come to be framed in terms of the risk characteristics of human capital. Rarely is the asset allocation decision integrated with life insurance decisions.

Motivated by the need to integrate these two decisions in light of the risk and return characteristics of human capital, we have analyzed these traditionally distinct lines of thought together in one framework. These two decisions must be determined jointly because they serve as risk substitutes when viewed from an individual investor's portfolio perspective.

Life insurance is a perfect hedge for human capital in the event of death. Term life insurance and human capital have a negative 100 percent correlation with each other. If one pays off at the end of the year, then the other does not, and vice versa. Thus, the combination of the two provides great diversification to an investor's total portfolio. **Figure 3.1** "updates" Figure 2.1 to illustrate the types of decisions the investor faces when jointly considering human capital, asset allocation, and life insurance decisions together with the variables that affect the decisions.

Figure 3.1.   Relationships among Human Capital, Asset Allocation, and Life Insurance

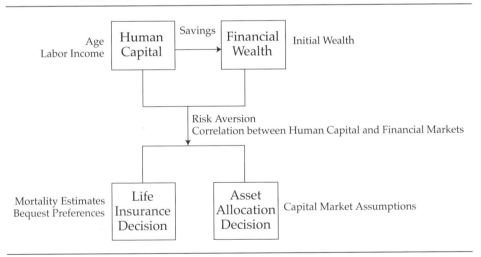

Human Capital, Life Insurance, and Asset Allocation

We discussed the literature on human capital and asset allocation extensively in Chapter 2, so in this chapter, we concentrate on the link between life insurance and human capital. A number of researchers have pointed out that the lifetime consumption and portfolio decision models need to be expanded to take into account lifetime uncertainty (or mortality risk). Yaari's 1965 paper is considered the first classical work on this topic. Yaari pointed out ways of using life insurance and life annuities to insure against lifetime uncertainty. He also derived conditions under which consumers would fully insure against lifetime uncertainty (see also Samuelson 1969; Merton 1969). Like Yaari, Fischer (1973) pointed out that earlier models either dealt with an infinite horizon or took the date of death to be known with certainty.

Theoretical studies show a clear link between the demand for life insurance and the uncertainty of human capital. Campbell (1980) argued that for most households, the uncertainty of labor income dominates uncertainty as to financial capital income. He also developed solutions based on human capital uncertainty to the optimal amount of insurance a household should purchase.[18] Buser and Smith (1983) used mean–variance analysis to model life insurance demand in a portfolio context. In deriving the optimal insurance demand and the optimal allocation between risky and risk-free assets, they found that the optimal amount of insurance depends on two components: the expected value of human capital and the risk–return characteristics of the insurance contract. Ostaszewski (2003) stated that life insurance—by addressing the uncertainties and inadequacies of an individual's human capital—is the business of human capital "securitization."

Empirical studies of life insurance adequacy have shown that underinsurance, however, is prevalent (see Auerbach and Kotlikoff 1991). Gokhale and Kotlikoff (2002) argued that questionable financial advice, inertia, and the unpleasantness of thinking about one's death are the likely causes.

Zietz (2003) has provided another excellent review of the literature on insurance.

Description of the Model

To merge considerations of asset allocation, human capital, and optimal demand for life insurance, we need a solid understanding of the actuarial factors that affect the pricing of a life insurance contract. Note that, although numerous life insurance product variations exist—such as term life, whole life, and universal life, each of which is worthy of its own financial analysis—we focus exclusively on the most fundamental type of life insurance policy—namely, the *one-year, renewable term policy*.[19]

On a basic economic level, the premium for a one-year, renewable term policy is paid at the beginning of the year—or on the individual's birthday—and protects the human capital of the insured for the duration of the year.[20] (If the insured person dies within that year, the insurance company pays the face value to the beneficiaries

---

[18]Economides (1982) argued in a corrected model that Campbell's approach underestimated the optimal amount of insurance coverage. Our model takes this correction into consideration.

[19]One-year, renewable term life insurance is used throughout this monograph. Appendix B provides a description of the pricing mechanism of this insurance policy. Although an analysis is beyond the scope of this monograph, we believe that all other types of life insurance policies are financial combinations of term life insurance with investment accounts, added tax benefits, and embedded options.

[20]In this description, we are obviously abstracting somewhat from the realities of insurance pricing, but to a first-order approximation, the descriptions capture the essence of actuarial cost.

soon after the death or prior to the end of the year.) Next year, because the policy is renewable, the contract is guaranteed to start anew with new premium payments to be made and protection received.

In this section, we provide a general approach to thinking about the joint determination of the optimal asset allocation and prudent life insurance holdings. Appendix B contains a detailed specification of the model that is the basis for the numerical examples and case studies later in the chapter.

We assume there are two asset classes. The investor can allocate financial wealth between a risk-free asset and a risky asset (i.e., bonds and stocks). Also, the investor can purchase a term life insurance contract that is renewable each period. The investor's objective is to maximize overall utility, which includes utility in the investor's "live" state and in the investor's "dead" state, by choosing life insurance (the face value of a term life insurance policy) and making an asset allocation between the risk-free and risky assets.[21] The optimization problem can be expressed as follows:

$$\max_{(\theta_x, \alpha_x)} E\left[(1-D)(1-\bar{q}_x)U_{alive}\left(W_{x+1}+H_{x+1}\right)+D(\bar{q}_x)U_{dead}\left(W_{x+1}+\theta_x\right)\right], \tag{3.1}$$

where

θ_x = amount of life insurance

α_x = allocation to the risky asset

D = relative strength of the utility of bequest, as explained in Appendix B

$\bar{q}_x$ = subjective probabilities of death at the end of the year $x+1$ conditional on being alive at age x

$1-\bar{q}_x$ = subjective probability of survival

W_{x+1} = wealth level at age $x+1$, as explained in Appendix B

H_{x+t} = human capital

and $U_{alive}(\cdot)$ and $U_{dead}(\cdot)$ are the utility functions associated with the alive and dead states. The model is repeated in Equation B.2 and described in detail in Appendix B.

We extend the framework of Campbell (1980) and Buser and Smith (1983) in a number of important directions. First, we link the asset allocation decision to the decision to purchase life insurance in one framework by incorporating human capital. Second, we specifically take into consideration the effect of the bequest motive (attitude toward the importance of leaving a bequest) on asset allocation and life insurance.[22] Third, we explicitly model the volatility of labor income and its correlation with the financial market. Fourth, we also model the investor's subjective survival probability.

---

[21]We assume that the investor makes asset allocation and insurance purchase decisions at the start of each period. Labor income is also received at the beginning of the period.

[22]Bernheim (1991) and Zietz (2003) showed that the bequest motive has a significant effect on life insurance demand.

Human capital is the central component that links both decisions. Recall that an investor's human capital can be viewed as a stock if both the correlation with a given financial market subindex and the volatility of the labor income are high. Human capital can be viewed as a bond if both the correlation and the volatility are low. In between those two extremes, human capital is a diversified portfolio of stocks and bonds, plus idiosyncratic risk. Again, we rely on some of the Davis–Willen (2000) parameters for our numerical case examples. It is important to distinguish between, on the one hand, correlations and dependence when considering human capital and aggregate stock market returns (such as return of the S&P 500 Index) and, on the other hand, correlations of human capital with individual securities and industries. Intuitively, a middle manager working for Dow Corning, for example, has human capital returns that are highly correlated with the performance of Dow Corning stock. A bad year or quarter for the stock is likely to have a negative effect on financial compensation.

The model has several important implications. First, as expressed in Equation 3.1, it clearly shows that both asset allocation and life insurance decisions affect an investor's overall utility; therefore, the decisions should be made jointly.[23] The model also shows that human capital is the central factor. The impact of human capital on asset allocation and life insurance decisions is generally consistent with the existing literature (e.g., Campbell and Viceira 2002; Campbell 1980). One of our major enhancements, however, is the explicit modeling of correlation between the shocks to labor income and financial market returns. The correlation between income and risky-asset returns plays an important role in both decisions. All else being equal, as the correlation between shocks to income and risky assets increases, the optimal allocation to risky assets declines, as does the optimal quantity of life insurance. Although the decline in allocation to risky assets with increasing correlation may be intuitive from a portfolio theory perspective, we provide precise analytic guidance on how it should be implemented. Furthermore, and contrary to intuition, we show that a higher correlation with any given subindex brings about the second result—that is, reduces the demand for life insurance. The reason is that the higher the correlation, the higher the discount rate used to estimate human capital from future income. A higher discount rate implies a lower amount of human capital—thus, less insurance demand.

---

[23]The only scenarios in which the asset allocation and life insurance decisions are not linked are when the investor derives his or her utility 100 percent from consumption or 100 percent from bequest. Both are extreme—especially the 100 percent from bequest.

©2007, The Research Foundation of CFA Institute

Second, the asset allocation decision affects well-being in both the live (consumption) state and the dead (bequest) state whereas the life insurance decision affects primarily the bequest state. Bequest preference is arguably the most important factor, other than human capital, in evaluating life insurance demand.[24] Investors who weight bequest as more important (who have a higher D) are likely to purchase more life insurance.

Another unique aspect of our model is the consideration of subjective survival probability, $1 - \bar{q}_x$. The reader can see intuitively that investors with low subjective survival probability (i.e., those who believe they have a high mortality rate) will tend to buy more life insurance. This "adverse selection" problem is well documented in the insurance literature.[25]

Other implications are consistent with the existing literature. For example, our model implies that the more financial wealth one has—all else being equal—the less life insurance one demands. More financial wealth also indicates more conservative portfolios when human capital is "bondlike." When human capital is "stocklike," more financial wealth calls for more aggressive portfolios. Naturally, risk tolerance also has a strong influence on the asset allocation decision. Investors with less risk tolerance will invest conservatively and buy more life insurance. These implications will be illustrated in the case studies.

We emphasize at this point that our analysis completely ignores the non-human-capital aspects of insurance purchases. For example, a wide variety of estate planning, business succession, and tax minimization strategies might increase demand for insurance much more than the level we have derived in our models. These aspects are beyond the scope of our analysis.

Case Studies

To illustrate the predictions of the model, we analyze the optimal asset allocation decision and the optimal life insurance coverage for five different cases. We solve the problem via simulation; the detailed solving process is presented in Appendix B.

For all five cases, we assumed the investor can invest in two asset classes. We used the capital market assumptions given in Table 2.1 of the previous chapter, which can be summarized as follows: compound annual geometric mean returns for bonds of 5 percent and for stocks of 9 percent, standard deviation of stock returns of 20 percent, and an inflation rate of 3 percent.

---

[24]A well-designed questionnaire can help elicit individuals' attitudes toward bequest, even though a precise estimate may be hard to obtain.

[25]The actuarial mortality tables can be taken as a starting point. Life insurance is already priced to take into account adverse selection.

In these case studies, the investor is female. Her preference toward bequest is one-fourth of her preference toward consumption in the live state.[26] She has no special information about her relative health status (i.e., her subjective survival probability is equal to the objective actuarial survival probability). Her income is expected to grow with inflation, and the volatility of the growth rate is 5 percent.[27] Her real annual income is $50,000, and she saves 10 percent each year. She expects to receive a Social Security payment of $10,000 each year (in today's dollars) when she retires at age 65. Her current financial wealth is $50,000. She is assumed to follow constant relative risk aversion (CRRA) utility with a risk-aversion coefficient of γ. Finally, we assume that her financial portfolio is rebalanced and the term life insurance contract renewed annually.[28] These assumptions remain the same for all cases. Other parameters, such as initial wealth, will be specified in each case.

Case #1. Human Capital, Financial Asset Allocation, and Life Insurance Demand over the Lifetime. In this case, we assumed that the investor has a CRRA, γ, of 4. Also, the correlation between the investor's income and the market return of the risky asset is 0.20.[29] For a given age, the amount of insurance this investor should purchase can be determined by her consumption/ bequest preference, risk tolerance, and financial wealth. Her expected financial wealth, human capital, and the derived optimal insurance demand over the investor's life from age 25 to age 65 are presented in **Figure 3.2**.

Several results of modeling this investor's situation are worth noting. First, human capital gradually decreases as the investor gets older and her remaining number of working years becomes smaller. Second, the amount of her financial capital increases as she ages as a result of growth of her existing financial wealth and the additional savings she makes each year. The allocation to risky assets decreases as the investor ages because of the dynamic between human capital and financial wealth over time. Finally, the investor's demand for insurance decreases as she ages. This result is not surprising because the primary driver of insurance demand is human capital, so the decrease in human capital reduces insurance demand.

These results appear to be consistent with conventional financial planning advice to reduce insurance holdings later in life, even though mortality risk itself has increased. In fact, one of the widespread misunderstandings about insurance, especially among young students of finance, is that a person needs large amounts

---

[26]That is, we set *D* equal to 0.2 in the model.

[27]The salary growth rate and the volatility were chosen mainly to show the implications of the model. They are not necessarily representative.

[28]The mortality and insurance loading is assumed to be 12.5 percent.

[29]Davis and Willen (2000) estimated the correlation between labor income and equity market returns by using the U.S. Department of Labor's "Current Occupation Survey." They found that the correlation between equity returns and labor income typically lies in the interval from −0.10 to 0.20.

Figure 3.2. Case #1: Human Capital, Financial Asset Allocation, and Insurance Demand over Lifetime

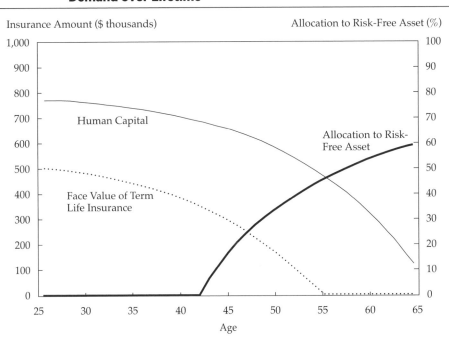

of life insurance only when facing the greatest chance of death (i.e., only for older people). To the contrary, the magnitude of loss of human capital at younger ages is far more important than the higher probability of death at older ages.

Case #2. Strength of the Bequest Motive. This case shows the impact of the bequest motive on the optimal decisions about asset allocation and insurance. In this case, we assume that the investor is age 45 and has an accumulated financial wealth of $500,000. The investor has a CRRA coefficient of 4. The optimal allocations to the risk-free asset and insurance for various bequest preferences are presented in **Figure 3.3**.

In this case, insurance demand increases as the bequest motive strengthens (i.e., as D gets larger). This result is expected because an investor with a strong bequest motive is highly concerned about her heirs and has an incentive to purchase a large amount of insurance to hedge the loss of human capital. In contrast, Figure 3.3 shows almost no change in the proportional allocation to the risk-free asset at different strengths of bequest motive. This result indicates that asset allocation is primarily determined by risk tolerance, returns on the risk-free and risky assets, and

Figure 3.3. Case #2: Optimal Insurance Demand and Allocation to the Risk-Free Asset by Strength of Bequest Preference

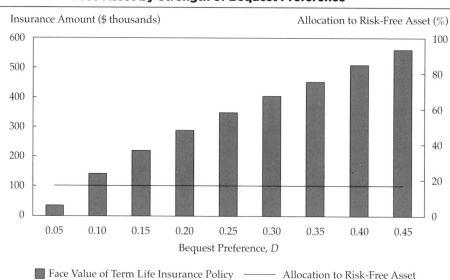

human capital. This case shows that the bequest motive has a strong effect on insurance demand but little effect on optimal asset allocation.[30]

Case #3. The Impact of Risk Tolerance.
In this case, we again assume that the investor is age 45 and has accumulated financial wealth of $500,000. The investor has a moderate bequest preference level (i.e., $D = 0.2$). The optimal allocations to the risk-free asset and the optimal insurance demands for this investor for various risk-aversion levels are presented in **Figure 3.4**.

As expected, allocation to the risk-free asset increases with the investor's risk-aversion level—the classic result in financial economics. Actually, the optimal portfolio is 100 percent in stocks for risk-aversion levels less than 2.5. The optimal amount of life insurance follows a similar pattern: Optimal insurance demand increases with risk aversion. For this investor with moderate risk aversion (a CRRA coefficient of 4) and the human and financial assumptions that we have made, optimal insurance demand is about $290,000, which is roughly six times her current income of $50,000.[31] Therefore, conservative investors should invest more in risk-free assets and buy more life insurance than aggressive investors should.

---

[30]In this model, subjective survival probability and the bequest motive have similar impacts on the optimal insurance need and asset allocation. When subjective survival probability is high, the investor will buy less insurance.

[31]This result is close to the typical recommendation made by financial planners (i.e., purchase a term life insurance policy that has a face value four to seven times one's current annual income). See, for example, Todd (2004).

Figure 3.4. Case #3: Optimal Insurance Demand and Allocation to the Risk-Free Asset by Risk-Aversion Level

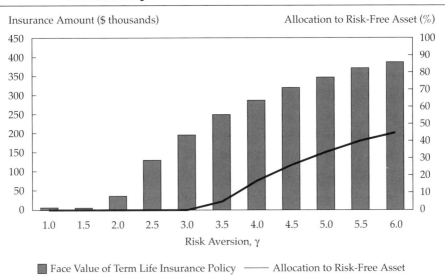

Insurance Amount ($ thousands)   Allocation to Risk-Free Asset (%)

Risk Aversion, γ

▮ Face Value of Term Life Insurance Policy ——— Allocation to Risk-Free Asset

Case #4. Financial Wealth.

For this case, we hold the investor's age at 45 and her risk preference and bequest preference at moderate levels (a CRRA coefficient of 4 and bequest level of 0.2). The optimal asset allocation to the risk-free asset and the optimal insurance demands for various levels of financial wealth are presented in **Figure 3.5**.

First, Figure 3.5 shows that the optimal allocation to the risk-free asset increases with initial wealth, which was discussed extensively in Chapter 2.

Second, optimal insurance demand decreases with financial wealth. This result can be intuitively explained through the substitution effects of financial wealth and life insurance. In other words, with a large amount of wealth in hand, one has less demand for insurance because the loss of human capital will have much less impact on the well-being of one's heirs. In Figure 3.5, the optimal amount of life insurance decreases from more than $400,000 when the investor has little financial wealth to almost zero when the investor has $1.5 million in financial assets.

In summary, for an investor whose human capital is less risky than the stock market, the more substantial the investor's financial assets are, the more conservative optimal asset allocation is and the smaller life insurance demand is.

Case #5. Correlation between Wage Growth Rate and Stock Returns.

In this case, we want to evaluate the life insurance and asset allocation decisions for investors with a high correlation between the risky asset and the investors' income. This kind of correlation can happen when an investor's income is closely linked to the stock performance of the company where the investor works

Figure 3.5. Case #4: Optimal Insurance Demand and Allocation to the Risk-Free Asset by Level of Financial Wealth

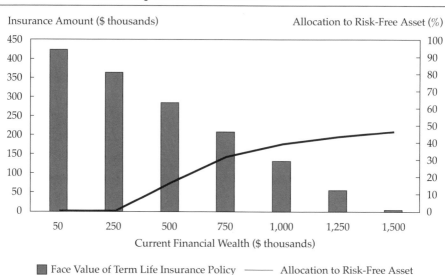

or when the investor's compensation is highly influenced by the financial market (e.g., the investor works in the financial industry).

Again, the investor's age is 45 and she has a moderate risk preference and bequest preference. Optimal asset allocation to the risk-free asset and insurance demand for various levels of correlations in this situation are presented in **Figure 3.6**.

The optimal allocation becomes more conservative (i.e., more allocation is made to the risk-free asset) as income and stock market return become more correlated, which is similar to the results described in Chapter 2. The optimal insurance demand decreases as the correlation increases. Life insurance is purchased to protect human capital for the family and loved ones. As the correlation between the risky asset and the income flow increases, the *ex ante* value of human capital to the surviving family decreases. This lower valuation on human capital induces a lower demand for insurance. Also, less money spent on life insurance indirectly increases the amount of financial wealth the investor can invest, so the investor can invest more in risk-free assets to reduce the risk associated with her total wealth.[32]

Another way to think about these results is to consider the certainty (or utility) equivalent of risky human capital, which can be thought of as the economic present value of a cash flow stream. The higher the correlation with other financial assets and the higher the volatility of the cash flow stream, the lower the certainty-equivalent value and, therefore, the lower the demand for insurance.

[32]See Case #3 for a detailed discussion of the wealth impact.

Figure 3.6. Case #5: Optimal Insurance Demand and Allocation to the Risk-Free Asset by Correlation Level

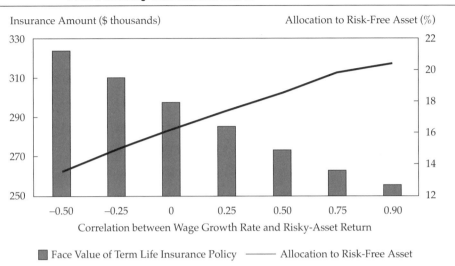

In summary, as wage income and stock market returns become more correlated, optimal asset allocation becomes more conservative and the demand for life insurance falls.

Summary

We have expanded on the basic idea that human capital is a "shadow" asset class that is worth much more than financial capital early in life and that it also has unique risk and return characteristics. Human capital—even though it is not traded and is highly illiquid—should be treated as part of a person's endowed wealth that must be protected, diversified, and hedged.

We demonstrated that the correlation between human capital and financial capital (i.e., whether the investor resembles more closely a bond or a stock) has a noticeable and immediate effect on the investor's demand for life insurance—in addition to the usual portfolio considerations. Our main argument is that the two decisions—quantity of life insurance and asset allocation—cannot be solved in isolation. Rather, they are aspects of the same problem.

We developed a unified human capital–based framework to help individual investors with both decisions. The model provided several key results:
- Investors need to make asset allocation decisions and life insurance decisions jointly.
- The magnitude of human capital, its volatility, and its correlation with other assets significantly affect the two decisions over the life cycle.

- Bequest preferences and a person's subjective survival probability have significant effects on the person's demand for insurance but little influence on the person's optimal asset allocation.
- Conservative investors should invest relatively more in risk-free assets and buy more life insurance.

We presented five case studies to demonstrate the optimal decisions in different scenarios.

4. Retirement Portfolio and Longevity Risk

In Chapters 2 and 3, we studied human capital and its impact on asset allocation and life insurance decisions for investors in the accumulation stage (i.e., when people are generally saving money prior to retirement). In the next three chapters, we shift our attention to the retirement stage.

In this chapter, we investigate the risk factors that investors face when making decisions about saving for and investing their retirement portfolios. We illustrate the common mistakes that investors experience when making their asset allocation and spending decisions in retirement. Through the use of Monte Carlo simulation techniques, we illustrate the longevity risk that investors face and the potential benefits of including lifetime-payout annuities in retirement portfolios.

Three Risk Factors in Retirement

A typical investor has two goals in retirement. The primary goal is to ensure a comfortable life style during retirement. In other words, investors would like to enjoy roughly the same life style in retirement that they had before (or a better one). Second, they would like to leave some money behind as a bequest. Three important risks confront individuals when they are making saving and investment decisions for their retirement portfolios: (1) financial market risk, (2) longevity risk, and (3) the risk of not saving enough (spending too much). Part of the third risk is the risk of inflation.

Financial Market Risk. Financial market risk, or volatility in the capital markets, causes portfolio values to fluctuate in the short run even though they may appreciate in the long run. If the market drops or corrections occur early during retirement, the individual's portfolio may not be able to weather the stress of subsequent systematic withdrawals. Then, the portfolio may be unable to generate the income necessary for the individual's desired life style or may simply run out of money before the individual dies.

Investors often ignore financial market risk by assuming a constant rate of return from their retirement portfolio (i.e., no market volatility). As a result, they make inappropriate asset allocations and product selections. For an illustration of the impact of the constant-return assumption, consider the following case. Assume that a 65-year-old investor has $1 million invested in a 60 percent stock/40 percent bond portfolio (hereafter, 60/40).[33] He would like to have $75,000 a year worth of income in retirement. Social Security and his defined-benefit (DB) pension plan will provide about $25,000 of this annual retirement income. Thus, he needs his investment portfolio to generate $50,000 each year from age 65 for the remainder of his life. Assuming that the compounded annual nominal returns for stocks and bonds are, respectively, 9 percent and 5 percent, the estimated average compounded annual nominal return on the portfolio is 7.4 percent. We assume inflation to be 3.0 percent.

Figure 4.1 shows the wealth and income levels projected for the constant returns in this case.[34] If we assume that the future return is constant, each year the portfolio will generate a 6.14 percent compounded return after expenses and fees, or roughly 3.14 percent after inflation. The $1 million portfolio will be able to sustain a withdrawal of more than $50,000 a year in real terms for the investor's life expectancy and beyond. In other words, with constant returns, the investor will meet his income needs and not run out of money.

Figure 4.1. Projected Wealth

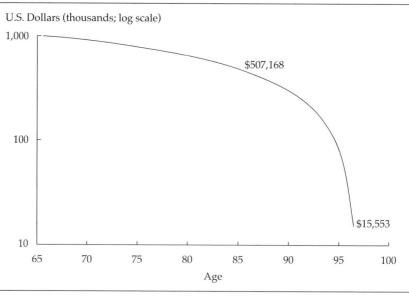

Note: 65-year-old male investor; $1 million; 60/40 portfolio.

---

[33] All dollar amounts presented in this chapter are in real dollars (i.e., inflation-adjusted amounts).
[34] All illustrations in this study are net of fees and expenses. Fee amounts were obtained from Morningstar Principia as of March 2006. They are 1.26 percent for mutual funds and 2.40 percent for variable annuities.

Market return, however, is not the same every year. In some periods, the portfolio returns will be much lower than 6.14 percent and may even be negative—as occurred in 2000, 2001, and 2002. So, although 6.14 percent may be a reasonable average assumption, it is unrealistic for the investor to make decisions based purely on the average return. Doing so underestimates the risk, and investors are generally risk averse by nature.

To show the impact of the entire return spectrum, we used a Monte Carlo simulation. Monte Carlo simulation is a technique to evaluate the outcome of portfolios over time by using a large number of simulated possible future return paths. In this case, the returns were randomly generated from a normal distribution with a 6.14 percent compounded average return and a 13 percent standard deviation.[35]

Panel A of **Figure 4.2** presents the Monte Carlo analysis results for the same case used in Figure 4.1. This analysis shows a 10 percent chance that this portfolio will be depleted by age 82, a 25 percent chance it will be depleted by age 88, and a 50 percent chance it will be depleted by age 95. When considered in light of the uncertain life spans of investors, this result reveals a much larger risk than many investors would accept. Panel B of Figure 4.2 shows the wealth produced by a nonannuitized 60/40 portfolio plus Social Security and DB plan payments of $25,000 a year.

Longevity Risk. Longevity risk is the risk of living longer than planned for and outliving one's assets. With life expectancies continuing to increase, retirees—especially those who retire early or have a family history of long lives—must be aware of the possibility of a long lifetime and adjust their plans accordingly.

Americans are living longer, on average, than ever before. The probability that an individual retiring at age 65 will reach age 80 is greater than 70 percent for females and greater than 62 percent for males. For a married couple, the odds reach nearly 90 percent that at least one spouse will live to age 70. As Figure 1.4 illustrated, in more than 80 percent of cases, at least one spouse will still be alive at age 85.

Simple retirement planning approaches ignore longevity risk by assuming the investor needs to plan only to age 85. It is true that 85 years is roughly the life expectancy for an individual who is 65 years old, but life expectancy is only the average estimate. Roughly half of investors will live longer than life expectancy. Therefore, investors who have used an 85-year life expectancy to plan their retirement income needs may find they have used up their retirement resources (other than government and corporate pensions) long before actual mortality. This longevity risk is substantial.

Risk of Spending Uncertainty. Investors may not save enough to adequately fund their retirement portfolios. Retirees are increasingly relying on investment income from their own portfolios, such as defined-contribution (DC) plans and individual retirement accounts, to fund their retirements. The ambiguity in this situation is that investors cannot determine exactly what they will earn between now and retirement. Moreover, they may not have the discipline to save adequately.

---

[35] In this study, we generated 2,000 return paths. Each path contained 35 years (from age 65 to age 100).

Figure 4.2. Nonannuitized Portfolio

A. Wealth

Wealth ($ thousands; log scale)

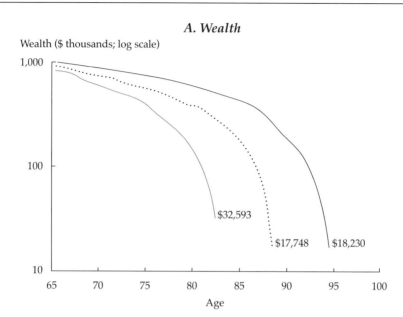

B. Annual Income

Income ($ thousands)

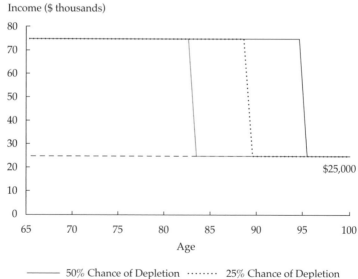

———— 50% Chance of Depletion   ········ 25% Chance of Depletion

———— 10% Chance of Depletion   – – – – Social Security and DB Payments

The evidence is that most investors do not save enough (Benartzi and Thaler 2001). A large proportion of investors do not even fund their 401(k) plans enough to use the match that their employers provide. If an employer provides a 50 percent match, then for each dollar an investor puts into her or his 401(k) plan, the employer puts in 50 cents. This immediate 50 percent "return" should not be given up by any rational employee, but it often is.

Although most savings can generate only normal capital market returns, savings are critical to meet retirement needs. To expect investment returns to compensate for a savings shortfall is not reasonable. To the contrary, investment returns allow the savings to multiply several times over the course of a retirement.

Controlling the Three Risks

Financial risk can be mitigated by using modern portfolio theory, which provides methods to reduce portfolio risk by capturing the long-term diversification benefits among investments. Insurance products can hedge away longevity risk. The risk of inadequate savings is primarily a behavioral issue.

For financial market risk, investors can turn to the rich literature and models of modern portfolio theory. Although financial market risk cannot be completely eliminated, investors can take advantage of the benefits of diversifying among various investments by following long-term asset allocation policies. The Markowitz mean–variance model is widely accepted as the gold standard for asset allocation.

Mean–variance optimization is a first step, but it considers only the risk and return trade-off in the financial market. It does not consider the longevity risk that people face during retirement.

DB pension plans provide longevity insurance by supplying their plan participants with income that cannot be outlived. In many cases, this income is also adjusted for inflation, which provides a further hedge against unexpected shocks to inflation. Fewer and fewer U.S. workers, however, are being covered by DB plans.

Because living a long life means needing more resources to fund longer-term income needs, rational investors will have to turn to sources other than DB plans. One approach is to take on more financial risk, if the investor can tolerate the risk, in the hopes of gaining more return. This plan can be accomplished by selecting an aggressive asset allocation policy (typically by using more stocks than the usual 60 percent and/or by adding higher-risk assets, such as hedge funds).

Rational investors will also want to hedge away the financial aspect of longevity risk because this type of risk exposure offers no potential reward.[36] In other words, investors should be willing to pay an insurance premium to hedge away the longevity risk. This approach is similar to the concept of homeowner insurance, which

---

[36]Living a long life is desirable, of course, from many aspects; we are focusing here only on the financial aspect of longevity.

protects against hazard to one's home. Lifetime annuities (payout annuities) provide investors with this type of longevity insurance. And lifetime annuities should be an integral part of many retirement plans precisely because of the real and substantial longevity risk—which should be treated just as seriously as the risks of disability, critical illness, and premature death.

Recently, behavioral economists have developed some innovative ways to help investors overcome the myopic behavior of spending today instead of saving for retirement. For example, Thaler and Benartzi (2004) pioneered the "Save More Tomorrow" (SMarT) program. SMarT takes advantage of the behavioral theory that people heavily weight current consumption over future (retirement) consumption. The program encourages workers to save some portion of their future *raises*, not their current income, in their 401(k) plans. In this plan, when they receive their raises, their savings rates go up but they still get to take home part of the extra compensation for immediate consumption. The plan is palatable because raises are in the future and people are less averse to trading future consumption for savings than to trading current consumption in order to save.

Longevity Risk and Sources of Retirement Income

Social security, DB pension plans, and personal savings (including DC savings) are the main sources of retirement income for Americans.[37] In this section, we look closely at the effectiveness of various sources in managing longevity risk.

Social Security and DB Pension Plans. Traditionally, Social Security and DB pension plans have provided the bulk of retirement income. For example, the U.S. Social Security Administration has reported that 39 percent of the income of persons 65 and older came from Social Security income in 2001 and 18 percent came from DB pensions (see GAO 2003). According to Employee Benefit Research Institute reports, current retirees receive about 60 percent of their retirement income from Social Security and traditional company pension plans, whereas today's workers can expect to have only about one-third of their retirement income funded by these sources (EBRI 2000).

Longevity insurance is embedded in U.S. government–funded Social Security and DB pension benefits because the benefits are paid out for as long as the beneficiary (and, typically, the beneficiary's spouse) lives. In DB pension plans, the employer (as plan sponsor) agrees to make future payments during retirement and is responsible for investing and managing the pension plan assets, thus bearing the investment and longevity risks. Because a DB pension plan typically covers a large number of employees, the overall longevity risk of the plan is significantly mitigated for the employer.

---

[37]Chapter 5 provides summary statistics on the sources of retiree income.

In the past two decades, a shift has been going on from DB plans to DC plans.[38] Over the past 20 years, the percentage of private-sector workers who participate in a DB plan has decreased and the percentage of such workers who participate in a DC plan has consistently increased. Today, the majority of active retirement plan participants are in DC plans, whereas most plan participants were in DB plans 20–30 years ago.

DC Plans and Other Personal Savings. Because workers increasingly must rely on their DC retirement portfolios and other personal savings as their primary sources of retirement income, workers must now bear longevity risk. DC plans contain no promise by an employer or the government that money will be available during retirement.

In addition to being exposed to longevity risk as never before, today's workers who are saving for retirement through DC plans have to manage this risk themselves. Personal savings are used to fund retirement income in two ways. First, a retiree may receive a lump sum directly from the plan as a cash settlement and then invest and withdraw from the portfolio during retirement. This plan is typically referred to as a "systematic withdrawal strategy." Second, a retiree may receive a lump sum and preserve the assets by purchasing a lifetime annuity with some or all of the proceeds to provide a stream of income throughout retirement. This plan is typically referred to as "annuitization."

Annuitization and systematic withdrawals (from an invested portfolio) have different advantages and risks for retirees. A life annuity, whether received from an employer-sponsored pension plan or purchased directly through an insurance company, ensures that a retiree will not run out of income no matter how long he or she lives. If a retiree dies soon after purchasing an annuity, however, he or she will have received considerably less than the lump sum a systematic withdrawal strategy would provide. With payout annuities, the investor will also be unable to leave that asset as a bequest, and the income from the annuity may not be adequate to pay for unexpected large expenses.

Retiring participants who systematically withdraw lump sums have the flexibility of preserving or drawing down those assets as they wish, but they risk running out of assets if they live longer than expected, if assets are withdrawn too rapidly, or if the portfolio suffers poor investment returns. Payout annuities offer a means to mitigate much of the financial uncertainty that accompanies living to a very old age but may not necessarily be the best approach for all retirees. For example, an individual with a life-shortening illness might not be concerned about the financial needs that accompany living to a very old age.

---

[38]The U.S. Department of Labor has reported that private-sector employers sponsored only approximately 56,000 tax-qualified DB plans in 1998, down from more than 139,000 in 1979. The number of tax-qualified DC plans sponsored by private employers more than doubled over the same period—from approximately 331,000 to approximately 674,000 (see GAO 2003).

Longevity Risk and Payout Annuities

Because mean–variance optimization addresses only the risk and return trade-offs in the financial markets, we focus our attention on the importance of longevity insurance. We touch on the difference between fixed- and variable-payout annuities and then move on to address the proper allocation of retiree income between conventional financial assets and payout annuity products that help to manage longevity risk.

Living a long life means more resources are needed to fund longer-term income needs. On the one hand, rational investors may decide to take on more financial risk in hopes of gaining more return. On the other hand, rational investors would also want to hedge away the financial aspect of longevity risk because there is no potential financial reward for this type of risk exposure. In other words, investors should be willing to pay an insurance premium to hedge away longevity risk. Lifetime-payout annuities provide investors with this type of longevity insurance.

A lifetime-payout annuity is an insurance product that converts an accumulated investment into income that the insurance company pays out over the life of the investor. Payout annuities are the opposite of life insurance. Investors buy life insurance because they are afraid of dying too soon and leaving family and loved ones in financial need. They buy payout annuities because they are concerned about living too long and running out of assets during their lifetime. Insurance companies can provide this lifelong benefit by spreading the longevity risk over a large group of annuitants and making careful and conservative assumptions about the rate of return to be earned on their assets.

Spreading or pooling the longevity risk means that individuals who do not reach their life expectancy (as calculated by actuarial mortality tables) subsidize those who exceed it. Investors who buy lifetime-payout annuities pool their portfolios and collectively ensure that everybody will receive payments as long as they live. Because of the unique longevity insurance features embedded in lifetime-payout annuities, they can play a significant role in many investors' retirement portfolios.

The two basic types of payout annuities are fixed and variable. A fixed-payout annuity pays a fixed nominal dollar amount each period. A variable annuity's payments fluctuate in accord with the performance of the fortunes of the underlying investments chosen by the buyer of the annuity. Payments from a lifetime-payout annuity are contingent on the life span of the investor. Other payout options are available, however, that might guarantee that payments will be made for a specified period of time or might offer refund guarantees. For examples, see Appendix C.

If an investor buys a life annuity from an insurance company, the investor is transferring the longevity risk to the insurance company, which is in a far better position than an individual to hedge and manage those risks. But of course, the investor pays a price. Should an investor self-insure against longevity risk?

Fixed-Payout Annuity. Figure 4.3 illustrates the payment stream from an immediate fixed annuity. With an initial premium or purchase amount of $1 million, the annual income payments for our 65-year-old male would be $6,910 a month, or $82,920 a year.[39] The straight line represents the annual payments before inflation. People who enjoy the security of a steady and predictable stream of income may find a fixed annuity appealing. The drawback of a fixed annuity, however, becomes evident over time. Because the payments are the same year after year, purchasing power is eroded by inflation as the annuitant grows older. The curved line in Figure 4.3 represents the same payment stream after taking into account a hypothetical 3 percent inflation rate.[40] Although the annuitant receives the same payment amount, that payment no longer purchases as much as it used to.

Figure 4.3. Income from Fixed Annuity

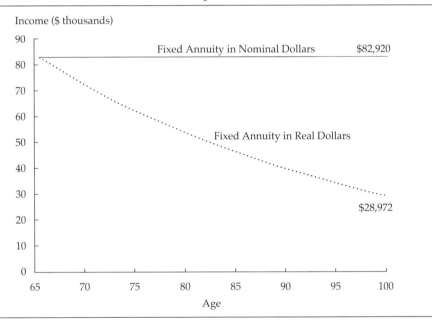

Despite the benefits of longevity insurance and fixed nominal payout amounts, a portfolio that consists solely of fixed lifetime annuities has several drawbacks. First, as noted, is decline in the value of the payments over time because of inflation. Second, one cannot trade out of the fixed-payout annuity once it has been

---

[39]This rate is the quote obtained in July 2006 for a 65-year-old male living in Illinois with $1 million to spend. The quote was obtained from www.immediateannuities.com.
[40]The average inflation rate in the United States from 1926 to 2006 was 3.04 percent.

purchased.[41] This aspect may be a problem for investors who need or prefer liquidity. Finally, when an investor buys a fixed annuity, the investor locks in payments based on the current interest rate environment. Payout rates from today's fixed-payout annuities are near historical lows because of current low interest rates. Our 65-year-old male might have received as much as $11,500 a month in the early 1980s in exchange for a $1 million initial premium. In 2003, that same $1 million bought only $6,689 a month. These drawbacks do not mean that fixed annuities are a poor investment choice. On the contrary, as we will show, fixed annuities can be a crucial part of a well-diversified retirement income portfolio.

Variable-Payout Annuities. A variable-payout annuity is an insurance product that exchanges accumulated investment value for annuity units that the insurance company pays out over the lifetime of the investor. The annuity payments fluctuate in value depending on the investments held; therefore, disbursements also fluctuate. To understand variable-payout annuities, think of a mutual fund whose current net asset value (NAV) is $1 per unit. The unit fluctuates each day. On any given day in any given week, month, or year, the price may increase or decrease relative to the previous period. With a variable annuity, instead of receiving fixed annuity payments, the investor receives a fixed number of fund units. Each month, the insurance company converts the fund units into dollars based on the NAV at the end of the month to determine how much to pay the investor. Therefore, the cash flow from the variable-payout annuity fluctuates with the performance of the funds the investor chooses.

Figure 4.4 illustrates the annuity payment stream, in real terms, from a 60/40 portfolio and a life-only payment option in an immediate variable annuity. We conducted a Monte Carlo simulation to illustrate the various payment scenarios. The simulation was generated for the case of the same investor discussed earlier from historical return statistics for stocks, bonds, and inflation for 1926–2006; a $1 million initial portfolio; and a 3 percent assumed investment return (AIR).[42] The initial payment at age 65 is estimated to be $66,153 a year.[43] The three lines in the chart show the 10th, 25th, and 50th percentiles. As Figure 4.4 demonstrates, there

---

[41]Payout annuities are available that do allow the investor to withdraw money from them, but the investor typically has to pay a surrender charge or market value adjustment charge. Furthermore, this flexibility applies only during the period of the annuity when payments are guaranteed regardless of life status.

[42]The AIR is an initial interest rate assumption that is used to compute the amount of an initial variable annuity payment. Subsequent payments will either increase or decrease depending on the relationship of the AIR to the actual investment return.

[43]All initial payments for immediate payout annuities were obtained from www.immediateannuity. com on 12 June 2005 for an assumed 65-year-old female living in Illinois and a $100,000 premium.

Figure 4.4. Income from 100 Percent Immediate Variable Annuity

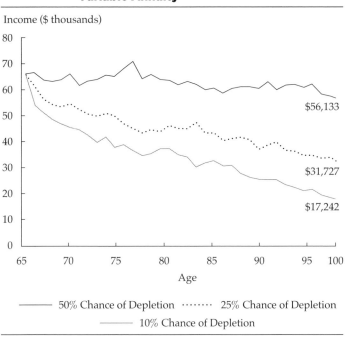

Income ($ thousands)

$56,133

$31,727

$17,242

50% Chance of Depletion ········ 25% Chance of Depletion

——— 10% Chance of Depletion

is a 10 percent chance that annual inflation-adjusted annuity payments will fall below $17,300 if the investor reaches 100, a 25 percent chance that they will be around $32,000 or lower, and a 50 percent chance that they will fall below $57,000.

Asset Allocation, Payout Annuities, and Disciplined Savings

Figure 4.5 shows the probability of success for two retirement income strategies— one using 100 percent systematic withdrawal from a 60/40 portfolio without any lifetime annuity (as depicted in Figure 4.1) and a second strategy using a payout annuity (25 percent fixed annuitization, 25 percent variable annuitization) and 50 percent systematic withdrawal from the same 60/40 portfolio. The systematic withdrawal strategy with no annuity has a higher risk of causing the portfolio to fall short of funding the required income need. The probability of success begins to drop before age 80 and falls to a low of 42 percent by age 100. The combination strategy is a far better strategy for increasing the odds of meeting income goals over this investor's lifetime. Although the probability of not being able to meet the income goal 100 percent of the time remains, the shortfall comes at a later stage in life and the success rate remains the highest.

Figure 4.5. Probability of Meeting Income Goal: Payout Annuities vs. Systematic Withdrawal

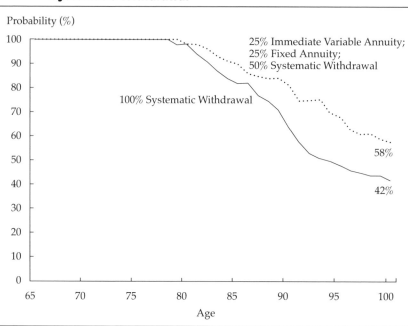

For retirees, such a combination of types of annuitization and systematic withdrawal could help manage the financial risks and the income needs they face during retirement. But what is the best combination of various types of annuities and systematic withdrawal? The next chapter explores the solution to the challenge of an asset allocation in retirement that includes both conventional asset classes and immediate payout annuity products.

Summary

In this chapter, we presented the three risk factors that investors face when making retirement portfolio decisions: financial market risk, longevity risk, and the risk of spending too much (which includes inflation risk). We focused on the role that lifetime-payout annuities should play in a retirement portfolio to alleviate both financial market and longevity risks. First, we demonstrated that traditional wealth-forecasting techniques that use a constant-return assumption can lead investors to believe they face little or no risk in funding retirement income needs. We then used a Monte Carlo simulation to illustrate more realistically the market risks in systematic withdrawal from a mutual fund portfolio, and we compared the results of withdrawal strategies with the benefits of payout annuities. Our analysis made clear that combining immediate fixed and variable life annuities with conventional investment instruments, such as mutual funds, is the optimal solution to providing retirement income.

This chapter demonstrated that an immediate payout annuity is an effective way to manage longevity risk in retirement. Buying a lifetime-payout annuitization is not, however, an all-or-nothing decision; the investor can choose how much to allocate between mutual fund accounts and annuitization. Combining nonannuitized assets with annuitized assets can help investors manage financial market risk, longevity risk, and bequest desires. In the next chapter, we present a model to develop an optimal asset allocation that includes fixed- and variable-payout annuities.

5. Asset Allocation and Longevity Insurance

In this chapter, we explore the idea of the optimal allocation to payout annuities in an investor's retirement portfolio. Our objective is to arrive at precise recommendations regarding how much of a retiree's portfolio income should contain longevity insurance in the form of pension (life) annuities and how much of the portfolio (and income) should be allocated to non-longevity-insured products, such as systematic withdrawal plans. The aim includes creating a comprehensive asset and product allocation strategy that addresses the unique requirements of today's, and tomorrow's, retirees.

As an investor ages, mortality risk (i.e., the risk that premature death will destroy the family's source of human capital) is replaced by longevity risk—the risk that the individual will outlive the time he or she has expected and planned to live. We argue that this risk also can be hedged by using an instrument that is the opposite of life insurance, namely, life annuities. In this chapter, we discuss how modern portfolio theory (MPT), which was originally designed for financial asset classes, can be merged with a similar framework for life annuities. We start by explaining the concept of mortality credit and then develop a simple one-period model with some numerical examples and some case studies. In Chapter 6, we delve in more detail into the optimal timing of annuitization.

In addition to the usual risk and return information from the financial markets, a model for the optimal demand for longevity insurance and life annuities requires inputs for the relative strength of the retiree's bequest motives, subjective health status, and liquidity restrictions. We discuss all of these in detail. Recall from earlier chapters that asset allocation is traditionally, in MPT, determined by constructing efficient portfolios for various risk levels (Markowitz 1952; Merton 1971). Then, based on the investor's risk tolerance, one of the efficient portfolios is chosen.

MPT is widely accepted as the primary tool for developing asset allocation recommendations. Its effectiveness is questionable, however, when dealing with asset allocations for individual investors in retirement because longevity risk is not considered in the classical framework. In this chapter, we review the need for longevity insurance during retirement and establish a framework for studying total asset allocation decisions in retirement, which includes conventional asset classes and immediate payout annuities.

Benefits of Longevity Insurance: Mortality Credits

Most retirees are hesitant to voluntarily purchase immediate annuities with their IRA (individual retirement account), 401(k), or other liquid wealth because they fear losing control and/or believe they can "do better" with other investment alternatives. Recent data from the LIMRA International research organization suggest that fewer than 5 percent of retirees who have a traditional variable annuity (VA) in accumulation choose to annuitize and derive income. When people within a traditional defined-benefit pension plan are offered the option of switching into a defined-contribution pension plan and giving up the implicit life annuity, most turn the offer down. Clearly, some confusion exists about the mechanics and benefits of these instruments. In the following section, we illustrate the benefits of annuitization and longevity insurance with a simple story, which also positions the income annuity product firmly within the realm of investment risk and return.

The 95-Year-Old Tontine Deal. Imagine five 95-year-old women who live in the United States and are interested in creating an investment club—but a club that is different from the usual kind. Each of the women invests $100 in a pool, but only survivors at the age of 96 can split the proceeds. While they are waiting to reach their 96th birthdays, the five women decide to put the money in a local bank's one-year certificate of deposit (CD) that is paying 5 percent interest for the year.

So, what will happen next year? According to statistics compiled by the U.S. Social Security Administration, there is a roughly 20 percent chance that a member of the investment club will die during the next year and, of course, an 80 percent chance that all will survive. And although virtually anything can happen to the women during the next 12 months of waiting, the probability implies that, *on average*, four 96-year-olds will survive to split the $525 pool at year end. Note that each survivor will receive $131.25 as her total return on the original investment of $100. The 31.25 percent investment return contains 5 percent of the bank's money and a healthy 26.25 percent of "mortality credits." These credits represent the capital and interest "lost" by the deceased and "gained" by the survivors.

The catch, of course, is that the *nonsurvivor* forfeits her claim to the funds. And although the heirs of the nonsurvivor's demise might be frustrated with the outcome, the survivors receive a superior investment return. More importantly, *all of them* are able to manage their lifetime income risk in advance without having to worry about what the future will bring. This story translates the benefits of longevity insurance into investment rates of return.

The story can be taken one step further. Suppose the investment club decides to invest the $500 in the stock market or some risky NASDAQ high-technology fund instead of a safe 5 percent CD for the next year. What happens if the value of the stock or high-tech fund falls 20 percent during the next year? How much will the surviving club members lose? If you think the answer is "nothing," you are absolutely correct. The four survivors divide the $400 among themselves so each receives her original $100 back.

Such is the power of mortality *credits*. They subsidize losses on the downside and enhance gains on the upside. In fact, one can argue that when adding longevity insurance to a diversified portfolio, an investor (or annuitant) can actually afford and tolerate more financial risk.

Of course, real life annuity contracts do not work in the way described in the story. Our hypothetical tontine contract is renewable each year, and the surviving 96-year-olds can take their mortality credits and go home. In practice, annuity contracts are for life and the mortality credits are spread and amortized over many years of retirement. The basic *insurance economics* of the annuity, however, are exactly as described for the hypothetical tontine. Chapter 6 will explore the mechanics and age-related effect of mortality credits, but for now, readers should keep in mind that mortality credits increase as the tontine members grow older.

The Payout Annuity's Insurance against Longevity Risk. The main lesson from the tontine story is that longevity risk can be hedged away with lifetime-payout annuities. A lifetime-payout annuity is an insurance product that exchanges an accumulated investment into payments that the insurance company pays out over a specified time—in this case, over the lifetime of the investor. Payout annuities are the exact opposite of traditional life (or more aptly named "premature death") insurance.

As discussed in Chapter 4, the two basic types of payout annuities are fixed annuities and variable annuities. A fixed-payout annuity pays a fixed dollar amount each period, perhaps with a cost-of-living adjustment, in real or nominal terms. A variable-payout annuity's payments fluctuate in value depending on the investments held, so disbursements also fluctuate. The payment from a lifetime-payout annuity is contingent on the life span of the investor. When the investor dies, his or her estate will no longer receive any payments unless a special guarantee period or estate benefit was purchased at the same time as the annuity. Such arrangements are normally paid for by reducing the benefit stream.

A substantial amount of literature has recently been written on the costs and benefits of life annuities. Space constraints prevent us from providing a comprehensive review, but the relevant academic literature can be roughly partitioned into three categories.

The first strand consists of literature on the theoretical insurance economics of life annuities. It investigates the equilibrium supply and demand of life annuities in the context of a complete market and utility-maximizing investors. This literature includes the classic work by Yaari (1965) and works by Richard (1975), Brugiavini

(1993), Yagi and Nishigaki (1993), and Milevsky and Young (2002). Broadly, the main conclusions of these investigators are that life annuities should play a substantial role in a retiree's portfolio.

The empirical annuity literature examines the actual pricing of these products and whether consumers are getting their money's worth when they buy life annuities. This strand includes a sequence of papers by Brown, Warshawsky, Mitchell, and Poterba in various combinations.[44]

A third and final strand is the attempt to create normative models to help investors decide how much to annuitize, when to annuitize, and the appropriate asset mix within annuities. These authors include Kapur and Orszag (1999), Blake, Cairns, and Dowd (2000), and Milevsky (2001).

We have tried to abstract from the complications one would encounter in reality by developing in this chapter a simple framework for analyzing the risk and return trade-off between one-period, tontine-like annuities and conventional asset classes.

Optimal Asset Allocation Mix with Payout Annuities

Smart asset allocation decisions that take advantage of the benefits of diversifying among different asset classes are an effective tool for managing and reducing market risk. Therefore, to help investors find the appropriate allocation of their savings in retirement, we must incorporate fixed- and variable-payout annuities into the traditional asset allocation models.

Classical asset allocation models used by popular software vendors and advisory services use information on the investor's time horizon and level of risk aversion to determine the appropriate asset mix. But to incorporate payout annuities and retirement dynamics in asset allocation, a proper model requires more information.

We have developed a model for optimally allocating investment assets within and between two distinct categories—annuitized assets and nonannuitized assets. The annuitized assets include fixed and variable immediate annuities. The nonannuitized assets could include all types of investment instruments—for example, mutual funds, stocks, bonds, and U.S. Treasury bills that do not contain a mortality-contingent income flow. In addition, a proper model must take into account the following decision factors:

- investor's risk tolerance,
- investor's age,
- investor's subjective probability of survival,
- objective probability of survival,
- relative weights the investor places on personal spending and creating an estate value, and
- risk and return characteristics of risky and risk-free assets.

---

[44]Poterba (1997); Mitchell, Poterba, Warshawsky, and Brown (1999); Brown and Poterba (2000); Brown (2001); Brown and Warshawsky (2001).

Regarding the trade-off between bequest (the desire to leave a bequest) and consumption (the need for liquidity in assets), the model developed in the next section incorporates classical economic models of consumer behavior. **Figure 5.1** provides a graphical illustration of the trade-off between the desire for bequest and liquidity needs in light of an existing pension income. The greater the desire for creating an estate, or the higher the bequest value, the lower the demand (or need for) payout annuities (PA). The reason is that life annuities trade off longevity insurance against the creation of an estate.

Figure 5.1. Trade-Off between Bequest and Consumption

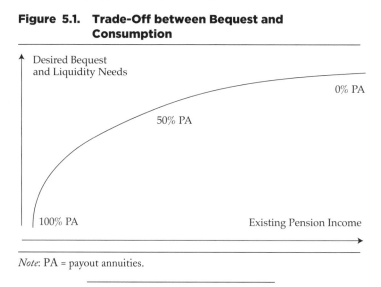

Note: PA = payout annuities.

Model Asset Allocation with Lifetime-Payout Annuities

We start by assuming that a rational, utility-maximizing investor is choosing the allocation of his retirement portfolio to maximize his utility. We also assume that the investor has four investment products to choose among: a risk-free asset, a risky asset, an immediate fixed annuity (IFA), and an immediate variable annuity (IVA). This model can be easily expanded to incorporate more assets.[45]

The model is formulated in a one-period framework, which makes the life annuity more of a tontine, but the underlying idea is the same regardless of the number of periods in the model. With four categories to choose from, the investor is looking at the traditional asset allocation problem. How does this rational, utility-maximizing individual go about selecting the right mix of risky and risk-free assets and of traditional financial instruments and immediate annuities?

---

[45]Chapter 5 is partly based on material in Chen and Milevsky (2003).

Table 5.1 summarizes the assumed returns from the four investment products conditioned on the alive state versus the dead state. From a mathematical point of view, we have the following problem: Find the asset allocation weights, denoted by a_1, a_2, a_3, a_4, that maximize the objective function

$$E[U(W)] = \bar{p} \times A \times E[U(a_1 wR + a_2 wX + a_3 wR/p + a_4 wX/p)]$$
$$+ (1 - \bar{p}) \times D \times E[U(a_1 wR + a_2 wX)], \tag{5.1}$$

subject to $a_1 + a_2 + a_3 + a_4 = 1$ and $a_i > 0$.

In this model, we use the following notation:

- A denotes the relative strength placed on the utility of consumption.
- D denotes the relative strength placed on the utility of bequest. The sum of A and D is assumed to be 1, so there is only one free variable. Individuals with no utility of bequest will be assumed to have $D = 0$.
- p denotes the objective probability of survival, which is the probability that is used by the insurance company to price immediate annuities.
- $\bar{p}$ denotes the subjective probability of survival. The subjective probability of survival may not match the objective (annuitant) probability. In other words, a person might believe he or she is healthier (or less healthy) than average. This circumstance would affect the expected utility but not the payout from the annuity, which is based on objective (annuitant) population survival rates.
- X denotes the (1 plus) random return from the risky asset.
- R denotes the (1 plus) risk-free rate.
- The expression $E[U(a_1 wR + a_2 wX + a_3 wR/p + a_4 wX/p)]$ denotes the utility from the live state.
- The expression $E[U(a_1 wR + a_2 wX)]$ denotes utility from the dead state. (Notice that the annuity term, which divides by the probability of survival, does not appear in the dead state because the annuity does not pay out in the dead state.)
- The function $U(\cdot)$ denotes the standard utility function for end-of-period wealth.

Table 5.1. Returns to Four Investment Choices

Asset	Alive State	Dead State
Risk-free asset (T-bills)	$R = 5\%$	$R = 5\%$
Risky asset (U.S. equity)	$X = 9\%$	$X = 9\%$
Immediate fixed annuity	$(1 + R)/p - 1$	0
Immediate variable annuity	$(1 + X)/p - 1$	0

Note: R = return to the risk-free asset, X = return to the risky asset, p = objective probability of survival.

The model can handle cases of both constant relative risk aversion (CRRA) and decreasing relative risk aversion as well as other functional forms that are consistent with loss aversion.

Because the weights a_1 through a_4 sum to 1, we essentially have only three weights to solve because $a_4 = 1 - (a_1 + a_2 + a_3)$. An important factor to consider in solving the utility maximization is that, as functions of (a_1, a_2, a_3), both $E[U(W)]$ and its derivatives are defined by integrals that cannot be performed analytically; they must be performed numerically.

The technical problem to be solved is to maximize the expected utility $E[U(W)]$ as a function of the weights a_1, a_2, and a_3, where $a_1 \geq 0$, $a_2 \geq 0$, $a_3 \geq 0$, and $a_1 + a_2 + a_3 \leq 1$. Now, although $E[U(W)]$ is a nonlinear function of the three free parameters (a_1, a_2, a_3), it is *strictly* concave; hence, one need only find a local maximum to find the global maximum.

Numerical Examples and Case Studies

To understand the intuition and results of the model, we examine several cases to gauge the effect of changing parameters on the optimal allocation. We start with the individual and capital market assumptions that will remain the same for all three cases. All cases will assume that the individual is a 60-year-old male who would like to allocate his portfolio among the two investment asset classes and the two mortality-contingent classes. The return, r_f, from the risk-free asset class (T-bills, termed "cash" in the tables and figure) is shown in Table 5.1 with no volatility. The return from the risky asset is lognormally distributed with a mean return value, R, of 9 percent and a standard deviation, SD, of 20 percent. (These return and risk assumptions are the same as those used for the cases studies in Chapters 2 and 3.)

For the objective mortality parameter, we use a table provided by the U.S. Society of Actuaries called the Individual Annuity Mortality (IAM) 2000 basic table. The basic table provides the probabilities of survival for a healthy population of potential annuitants. The subjective probability of survival may be lower (or higher) than the numbers indicated by the IAM 2000. The utility preferences are taken from the CRRA family, with a CRRA coefficient of γ. Finally, a 20-year horizon represents the one period. In other words, the individual intends to reallocate (rebalance) assets after 20 years. In practice, of course, investors should rebalance their portfolios much before the 20-year horizon, which requires a dynamic, multiperiod model.

Case #1. Total Altruism and Complete Bequest Motive. In this case, the investor's utility is derived entirely from bequests. That is, the weight of his utility of bequest is assumed to be 1 and the weight of his utility of consumption is 0: $D = 1$ and $A = 0$. The objective probability of survival is 65 percent (roughly equal to the survival probability of a 60-year-old male in the next 20 years), and

the subjective probability is the same 65 percent. In other words, we are assuming that the investor does not have any private information about his or her mortality status that would lead him to believe he is healthier or less healthy than average men of his age.

Based on these input parameters, the model produces the optimal allocations, by risk aversion, given in **Table 5.2**.

Table 5.2. Optimal Allocations for Case #1: Complete Bequest Motive

Risk Aversion	Cash	Equity	IFA	IVA	Total Risk Free	Total Risky	Total Traditional	Total Annuity
1.0	0%	100%	0%	0%	0%	100%	100%	0%
1.5	0	100	0	0	0	100	100	0
2.0	21	79	0	0	21	79	100	0
2.5	37	63	0	0	37	63	100	0
3.0	49	51	0	0	49	51	100	0
3.5	57	43	0	0	57	43	100	0
4.0	63	37	0	0	63	37	100	0
4.5	68	32	0	0	68	32	100	0
5.0	71	29	0	0	71	29	100	0
5.5	74	26	0	0	74	26	100	0
6.0	76	24	0	0	76	24	100	0

Notes: Male, age = 60, 65 percent objective and subjective survival probability, 100 percent bequest, 20-year horizon, R_f = 5 percent, $\bar{R}$ = 9 percent, SD = 20 percent. In the column headings, IFA stands for immediate fixed annuity and IVA stands for immediate variable annuity.

A few things are evident from Table 5.2. First, immediate annuities receive no allocation because the investor cares only about leaving a bequest. The intuition for this result can be traced back to a classic paper by Yaari (1965). If consumers are 100 percent altruistic, they will not waste the asset by annuitizing. Second, the allocation to stocks gradually decreases as the investor's risk aversion increases. Thus, because the investor has no consumption motive, the allocation task is the traditional choice of risk-free versus risky assets. For example, for investors with a relative risk-aversion level of 2, the optimal allocation is 21 percent to the risk-free asset and 79 percent to equity.

This case can be viewed as an illustration for extraordinarily wealthy individuals for whom the size of the portfolio far exceeds consumption needs. For such individuals, bequest becomes the dominant factor. Annuities do not receive any allocation because longevity insurance is not needed and annuities prevent leaving any money to heirs.

Case #2. No Bequest Motive. This case maintains the same age and gender, survival probability, and time horizon but completely eliminates the strength of bequest; that is, $A = 1$ and $D = 0$. In other words, 100 percent of the utility weight is placed on "live" consumption. The optimal allocations to the assets among various risk-aversion levels are presented in **Table 5.3**.

Table 5.3. Optimal Allocations for Case #2: No Bequest Motive

Risk Aversion	Cash	Equity	IFA	IVA	Total Risk Free	Total Risky	Total Traditional	Total Annuity
1.0	0%	0%	0%	100%	0%	100%	0%	100%
1.5	0	0	0	100	0	100	0	100
2.0	0	0	21	79	21	79	0	100
2.5	0	0	37	63	37	63	0	100
3.0	0	0	49	51	49	51	0	100
3.5	0	0	57	43	57	43	0	100
4.0	0	0	63	37	63	37	0	100
4.5	0	0	68	32	68	32	0	100
5.0	0	0	71	29	71	29	0	100
5.5	0	0	74	26	74	26	0	100
6.0	0	0	77	23	77	23	0	100

Note: Male, age 60, 65 percent survival, 0 percent bequest, 20-year horizon, $R_f = 5$ percent, $R = 9$ percent, $SD = 20$ percent.

Because the returns on annuities are always higher than the returns on traditional assets—conditional on the retiree being alive—the immediate annuities receive 100 percent of the allocation in this case. The allocation to the immediate variable annuity gradually decreases, whereas the allocation to the immediate fixed annuity increases as the risk aversion of the investor increases.

This case can be used as an illustration for investors who would like to maximize their lifetime consumption and have no interest in leaving any money behind. (They are sometimes known as the "die broke" crowd.) All the savings should be used to purchase annuities. Overall, the optimal allocation between risky and risk-free assets (in this case, they are an immediate fixed annuity and an immediate variable annuity) is almost identical to that of Case #1. For investors with a risk-aversion level of 2, for example, the optimal allocation is 21 percent to the immediate fixed annuity and 79 percent to the immediate variable annuity.

Case #3. Bequest Motive of 20 Percent and Consumption Motive of 80 Percent. In this variation, the strength of the bequest motive is raised from $D = 0$ to a more realistic $D = 0.2$. In other words, 80 percent of the utility weight is placed on alive-state consumption. The optimal allocations to the assets for various risk-aversion levels are presented in **Table 5.4**. **Figure** 5.2 depicts the allocations graphically.

Table 5.4.   Optimal Allocations for Case #3: Bequest Motive 20 Percent, Consumption Motive 80 Percent

Risk Aversion	Cash	Equity	IFA	IVA	Total Risk Free	Total Risky	Total Traditional	Total Annuity
1.0	0%	34%	0%	66%	0%	100%	34%	66%
1.5	0	50	0	50	0	100	50	50
2.0	13	48	8	31	21	79	61	39
2.5	25	42	12	20	37	63	67	33
3.0	35	37	14	14	49	51	72	28
3.5	43	33	14	10	57	43	76	24
4.0	50	29	13	8	63	37	79	21
4.5	55	26	13	6	68	32	81	19
5.0	59	24	12	5	71	29	83	17
5.5	62	22	12	4	74	26	84	16
6.0	65	20	11	3	76	24	86	14

Note: Male, age 60, 65 percent survival, 20 percent bequest, 20-year horizon, R_f = 5 percent, R = 9 percent, SD = 20 percent.

Figure 5.2.   Optimal Allocations: Bequest Motive 20 Percent, Consumption Motive 80 Percent

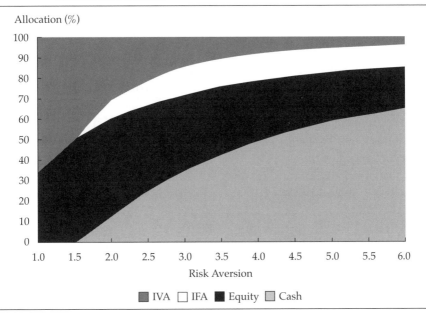

There are several interesting allocation results in this case. First, unlike the previous two cases, all four of the asset classes are represented in the optimal allocations. The reason is that immediate annuities are more suitable than traditional assets for consumption and traditional investments are more suited for bequest motives in this one-period framework. In general, the higher the bequest motive of an investor, the more the investor should allocate to traditional investments and the less to immediate annuities.

Second, the allocations between risky (both IVA and equity) and risk free (cash and IFA) are almost identical to those in Case #1 and Case #2 at comparable risk-aversion levels. This result indicates that the changes in the investor's bequest and consumption motives do not have a significant impact on the investor's behavior regarding risk. The optimal allocation between risky and risk-free assets is determined by the investor's risk tolerance.

Third, the allocation to annuities decreases as the investor's risk aversion increases. In other words, investors who are more averse to market risk will avoid immediate life annuities. This outcome makes intuitive sense: The investor can get little or no utility from immediate annuity investments if he or she dies shortly after the purchase. With traditional investments, some utility will be left for the heirs. Apparently, the higher aversion to market risk increases the implicit weight on the utility of bequest. For an investor with a risk-aversion level of 2, the optimal allocation is 13 percent cash, 48 percent equity, 8 percent IFA, and 31 percent IVA.

Summary

This chapter was motivated by investors' need to manage longevity risk together with financial risk. We introduced a model that merges financial market risk *and* longevity risk in analyzing the economic trade-off of investments.

Our main qualitative insight is as follows. The natural asset allocation spectrum consists of investments that go from safe (fixed) to risky (variable). The product allocation spectrum ranges from conventional savings vehicles to annuitized payout (pension) instruments. The asset and product spaces are separate dimensions of a well-balanced financial portfolio; yet, the product/asset allocation must be analyzed jointly.

Formally, we presented a mathematical one-period model to analyze the optimal allocations within and between payout annuities and traditional asset classes. The numerical results confirm that the optimal allocations among assets are influenced by such factors as age, risk aversion, subjective probability of survival, utility of bequest, and the expected risk and return trade-offs of various investments. We also found that the global allocation between risky and risk-free assets is influenced only by the investor's risk tolerance; it is not significantly affected by the subjective probability of survival or the utility of consumption versus the utility of bequest.

In some sense, we are advocating a classical economic "separation theorem" argument. The first step of a well-balanced retirement plan is to locate a suitable global mix of risky and risk-free assets independently of the assets' mortality-contingent status. Then, once a comfortable balance has been struck between risk and return, the annuitization decision should be viewed as a second-step "overlay" that is placed on top of the existing asset mix. And depending on the strength of the investor's bequest motives and subjective health assessments, the optimal annuitized fraction will follow. These assume that the payout annuities contain only longevity insurance without any other options (i.e., benefit riders).

Of course, retirement is not one point or period in time. In the next chapter, we analyze the impact of aging on the optimal timing of annuitization.

6. When to Annuitize

In Chapters 4 and 5, we made the point that payout annuities, either variable or fixed, have a rightful place in an individual investor's optimal retirement portfolio.[46] We argued that, depending on an individual investor's bequest motive versus the investor's desire for consumption, the investor should have a substantial portion of total wealth allocated to annuities that provide some form of guaranteed income for life.

The same principles that govern the allocation of financial assets should govern product allocation. For example, as much as 75 percent of desired (retirement) income can and should be longevity insured. Of course, for those investors with lucrative defined-benefit (DB) pensions and/or Social Security benefits, a large portion of retirement income may already contain longevity insurance. These investors have no need to acquire more. Individuals who do not have longevity insurance prior to retirement, however, should be interested in acquiring some protection against outliving their resources.

Table 6.1 illustrates the extent to which Americans' retirement income is currently longevity insured. A typical retiree has diverse sources of income. Many are entitled to a Social Security payment, a number of them have DB pensions, and some have income from other annuities. All of these assets are longevity insured; they cannot be outlived, although their real purchasing power might decline over time. Other sources of retirement income, such as employment, interest income, dividends, and systematic withdrawal from market funds, are not longevity insured. Note from Table 6.1 that at advanced ages, 80 percent of an average retiree's income is longevity insured. And although these numbers are population averages, they do confirm that longevity insurance is not an esoteric concept. For the average American, longevity-insured assets are the foundation of his or her retirement income. Another pattern in Table 6.1 is that as the age in the U.S. retiree age group decreases, so does the percentage of income that contains longevity insurance, probably as a result of the reduced coverage of U.S. workers by DB pension plans.

In light of the dwindling longevity insurance shown in Table 6.1, the question—and the focus of this chapter—is exactly *when* and *how* individual investors should go about purchasing income annuities or longevity insurance policies if they do not have them already. Intuitively, purchasing an (irreversible) immediate income annuity at the age of 30, 40, or even 50 makes little sense for a variety of reasons. First of

---

[46]See related papers by Chen and Milevsky (2003) and Ameriks, Veres, and Warshawsky (2001). For more theoretical papers that made the same arguments, see the classic by Yaari (1965) and the recent extension by Davidoff, Brown, and Diamond (2005).

Table 6.1. Average Longevity-Insured Portion of Income for U.S. Population, 2004

Age Group	Portion Insured
65–69	49.9%
70–74	62.4
75–79	70.4
80–84	75.1
85+	80.1

Note: Longevity-insured assets are Social Security, DB pensions, and annuities.

Source: Employee Benefit Research Institute (EBRI 2006).

all, the mortality credits—the *raison d'être* of annuitization, which we explained in Chapter 5—are miniscule at these ages. Moreover, real world transaction costs, fees, and expenses would easily eliminate the effect of mortality-insurance pooling. The empirical data tell the same story as our intuition: The implied longevity yields from payout annuities computed at the age of 50 by the methodology developed in Milevsky (2005b) are substantially lower than the relevant risk-free rates.

Here is a slightly more rigorous way to think about this issue. At the age of 50, the unisex mortality rate (i.e., the probability of a man or woman dying within one year) in the United States is approximately 0.4 percent, or 4 deaths per 1,000 people in that age group, according to the Retirement Pension (RP) 2000 (pensioners, nonprojected) mortality table provided by the Society of Actuaries. Thus, if the underlying pricing interest rate for the annuity in the economy is 5 percent, then annuitization at age 50 would add only 42 bps of return (i.e., mortality credits). These mortality credits are relatively insensitive to the pricing rate or the underlying interest rate in the economy. At a 7 percent pricing rate, the mortality credits would be 43 bps, and at a 10 percent pricing rate, they would be 44 bps. In fact, to a crude first order of approximation, the mortality credits are slightly higher than the mortality rates themselves, as per the following Taylor series expansion:

$$\text{Mortality credits} = \frac{1+R}{1-q_x} - (1+R) \approx q_x(1+q_x) + Rq_x(1+q_x) > q_x, \tag{6.1}$$

where R denotes the pricing rate and q_x is the mortality credit at age x.

Moreover, although an additional 42 bps of investment return is not something to be taken lightly, few of these mortality credits are likely to accrue to the annuitant (or tontine participant) once insurance company profits, commissions, and transaction costs are taken into account. More importantly, any insurance company that must set aside equity capital on the order of 5–10 percent of annuity reserves will demand a return on equity on the order of 10–20 percent, which creates a drag of yet another 50–200 bps, even for the most efficient, low-cost providers unless they are not-for-profit organizations or, perhaps, a government entity. Moreover, if we consider the Individual Annuity Mortality (IAM) 2000 basic table instead of the higher mortality rates (i.e., less antiselection) in the RP2000 table, the pure mortality credits at age 50 drop to about 30 bps.[47]

Table 6.2 displays the mortality credits at increasing ages under the assumption of a unisex mortality table that averages the q values in Equation 6.1 with a 40 percent weight to male mortality and a 60 percent weight to female mortality. These numbers were generated from the annuitant mortality table (the RP2000), which includes the antiselection effect one would experience with such a group. Notice how only after age 65 do the credits exceed 100 bps. Note also that at higher ages, they are substantial.

Table 6.2. Value of Unisex Mortality Credits

Age of Annuitant	Spread above Pricing Interest Rate
55	35 bps
60	52
65	83
70	138
75	237
80	414
85	725
90	1,256
95	2,004
100	2,978

Note: Assuming a 40 percent weight to male mortality and a 60 percent weight to female mortality; 6 percent net interest.

Source: The IFID Centre calculations.

Mortality credits can also be viewed as the threshold investment return required to beat the income from the annuity during the year in question. If a so-called self-annuitizer can earn the pricing rate, R, plus whatever is left of the mortality credits in Equation 6.1 after transaction costs, the person is better off not annuitizing at age 50 but waiting until age 51 to consider the decision. The following equation makes this point algebraically:

$$a_{x+1} = a_x \left(\frac{1+R}{1-q_x} \right) - 1, \tag{6.2}$$

---

[47]Remember that a large number of mortality tables are used by actuaries in the insurance industry. The RP2000 table is meant to capture the behavior (i.e., mortality) of general members of a DB pension plan, whereas the IAM tables are meant to cover a (healthier) group of individuals who tend to purchase life annuities.

where the actuarial symbol a_x denotes the annuity factor, or the cost of $1 of income per year for life starting at age x, under a valuation rate of R. Similarly, a_{x+1} denotes the annuity factor at age $x + 1$.

Equation 6.2 is an actuarial identity based on the definition of the annuity factor. From a financial point of view, it implies the following: If the quantity a_x can be invested to earn a total return of $(1 + R)/(1 - q_x)$ or greater, the investor at age x can consume the same dollar the annuity would have provided and still have enough funds to purchase an identical income annuity at age $x + 1$, under the assumption the q and R values do not change from one year to the next. In that case, why would the investor ever annuitize at the age of x?

Thus, when the individual investor has no bequest motive (i.e., does not care about leaving any inheritance) and experiences zero transaction costs, he or she should definitely annuitize at age 50 (or even earlier) simply to gain access to the 42 bps, despite its meagerness. But in the real world, this situation never happens. Although a 50-year-old investor may claim to have no bequest motives, the investor's preferences may change over the remaining 30–40 years of his or her life. Annuitizing totally at age 50 kills the option of acting on any bequest preference that develops.

Another problem with premature annuitization is that when the immediate annuity is of the fixed nominal (or even real) type—which currently represents 90 percent of income annuities sold in the United States—the individual investor is selecting an *asset allocation* together with an annuitization *allocation*.[48] The asset class underlying the annuity is essentially fixed-income assets with a predetermined duration and sensitivity to interest rates. This is precisely where the irreversible nature of real world annuities, as opposed to pure tontines, affects the optimal age and process by which to annuitize. Given that this contract is for life, the annuitant must now commit to a fixed-income asset allocation that can never be altered. A typical investor would surely want to rebalance and reallocate wealth to different asset classes over time, but the locked-in nature of the contract impedes the ability to rebalance.

An inability to rebalance is costly from a utility perspective and reduces the appeal of annuitization at all ages, as argued by Browne, Milevsky, and Salisbury (2003). Stated differently and in the language of Equation 6.1, although we would like to gain access to the mortality credit portion, q_x, we might not desire the return, R, that comes with it.

Indeed, in a perfect world, one could offset, hedge, or strip away the undesired exposure to bonds by shorting an appropriate fixed-income portfolio with an equal and opposite duration, but for the simple individual investor, the transaction costs

---

[48] According to LIMRA International estimates, approximately $150 million of retail premiums [not including the 403(b) market] went to variable-income annuities and approximately $2 billion went to fixed-income annuities in 2004.

would be prohibitive. By annuitizing prematurely into a fixed immediate annuity, not only are investors forced into an undesired bond allocation today, but they are forced to maintain this suboptimal allocation for the rest of their natural lives. Consider, for example, an investor who rationally wants to maximize her discounted lifetime utility by holding 100 percent equities—or given the hedging characteristics of human capital, perhaps even more—in her personal portfolio. Forcing her to hold bonds, even with the ongoing mortality credits, might be worse for her in a utility-adjusted sense than for her to hold the desired equities without the mortality credits.

In fact, even when an individual investor has access to low-cost immediate variable annuities that can be rebalanced among a variety of traditional asset class, such as stocks, bonds, cash, real estate, and commodities, an inherent loss of flexibility comes from restricting choices to a given company's family of investment accounts—which is an inevitable by-product of real world annuities.

All utility-destroying restrictions negate the mortality credits at younger ages. This point has recently been made rigorously by Milevsky and Young (2007). They found little theoretical justification for annuitization prior to the ages of 65–70.

Financial economists and pension economists who argue the benefits of annuities and their mortality credit subsidies, as per Equation 6.1, are really discussing pure tontines that can be renegotiated at the end of some arbitrary and fictitious time period. These products—if they actually existed—would contain the *real option* to change one's mind, preferences, and strategy at the end of the period.

A related issue is annuitizing at a young age but with income payments starting at an advanced age.[49] Is this akin to annuitizing prematurely, or is it enough that income starts at an advanced age? Would the same logic apply as in the case of mortality credits?

If the delayed annuity is 100 percent reversible (i.e., the investor can cash out at market value at any time prior to the income commencement date), then we would argue that annuitization has not really taken place. The purchase of the delayed annuity at age 30, 40, or even 50 is effectively a fixed-income allocation with an embedded call option to annuitize. The call option's underlying state (stochastic) variable is the changing mortality tables used to price annuities or population hazard rate (rate of mortality). Because the investor can fully reverse the decision, possibly subject to a market value adjustment based on the new level of interest rates, no pooling of mortality risk occurs until the income annuity begins paying. The value of the embedded call option to annuitize—hence, the relative appeal of this type of product compared with a straight bond—would depend critically on the specifics, such as the implied mortality rates in the contract relative to current annuity rates. The devil is in the details, and it is impossible to pass

---

[49]Several insurance companies have rolled out products that allow investors to annuitize at a young age but with payment starting at an older age.

judgment on the relative merits of such a product in the absence of the contract parameters.[50] Is the mortality table fixed at the time of purchase or dependent on population mortality at the time of annuitization? Is the strike price of this option to annuitize currently in the money or far out of the money? At best, it could be a surrogate for a desired bond allocation; at worst, it would be an overpriced and unnecessary call option.

In fact, we would argue that a traditional DB pension plan is effectively a staggered purchase of fixed-income strips, plus the mortality call options. (Even if the delayed annuity is not cashable in a mark-to-market sense, as long as there is some cash value that accrues over time and can be accessed at some point—perhaps at death, disability, or retirement—the same comments would apply.) Oddly, what we are saying is that an investor in a DB pension plan is not really accruing or accumulating income annuities but, rather, is buying an option to annuitize based on some mortality table. The decision to annuitize takes place at retirement when the retiree decides to *not* take the lump sum option, which is available in most DB pension plans.

Now, in contrast, if the delayed annuity is 100 percent irreversible with zero cash value and no survivor benefit, then we would concede that to start accumulating these credits at a young age might be optimal, provided the concerns about transaction costs did not negate the mortality credits. This concept is the advanced-life delayed annuity product explored in Milevsky (2005a). In this approach, a small premium is paid on an ongoing basis in exchange for a mortality-contingent income that starts at an advanced age. Note, however, that the threshold for beating the implied return from the delayed annuity at younger ages would still be quite low, even if the income did not start until an advanced age. Another factor to consider would be the embedded option on a given mortality table (i.e., the commitment to use current rates regardless of what happens to aggregate mortality), which might also increase the relative value of such a strategy/product. Again, the devil is in the details, so generalizing about the merits of such products is quite difficult, especially after taking into account fees, commissions, and profit margins.

Thus—despite the preponderance of theoretical arguments in favor of annuitization—we are hesitant to advocate a single optimal age at which an investor should convert his or her savings account into an irreversible income annuity. Given the many trade-offs involved in this decision and numerous sources of uncertainty, we *are* comfortable with suggesting that prior to age 60 is too early whereas waiting until the age of 90 is too late. (At the advanced age of 90, the unisex mortality rate, q_{90}, of 15 percent leads to mortality credits of 1,850, which are insurmountable on any investment frontier.)

---

[50] See the paper by Milevsky and Abaimova (2005) for an attempt to analyze a type of product that offers this call option in defined-contribution pension plans.

For these reasons, a body of literature is emerging that suggests that investors should annuitize slowly, as in a dollar-cost-averaging (DCA) strategy.[51] Depending on contract and policy features, this process would start at, for example, age 65–70 and continue until age 80 or 85, until the entire amount of desired annuity income was actually annuitized. Milevsky and Young (2007) proved the optimality of a staggered purchase option that annuitizes a small fraction on an ongoing basis. That result does not come from any attempt to speculate on interest rates or to time the shape of the yield curve. Rather, it is the natural result of balancing out the competing risks we described earlier.

There are two exceptions to this general rule, however, although both are rare. One is a situation in which long-term interest rates are extraordinarily high. The second may occur if consumers have solid reasons to believe that they are much healthier than the average annuitant. Of course, that judgment will be harder for people to make than whether they are much healthier than other people of the *same age*.

In summary, a number of previous research papers have been devoted to emphasizing the important role of income/payout annuities in the optimal portfolio of an individual investor. We have repeated the arguments that allocation to income annuities (and insurance) is just as important as allocation to financial instruments—stocks, bonds, cash, and so on. The theoretical arguments in favor of annuitization are so powerful that an entire body of economic literature has emerged under the title of "the annuity puzzle" that seeks to discover the reasons so few consumers actively and consciously embrace these instruments. Nevertheless, we remain unsure of the precise age at which this product allocation should take place. All we can offer is a range.

Additional reasons exist to delay annuitization. First, the retiree maintains complete control of her funds, which means that she maintains liquidity. She can meet emergencies or unforeseen cash crunches—for long-term care, for example—from a nonannuitized pool of money. Second, the retiree retains the option to annuitize at some later time. Why pay for something today if you can probably pay for it in 10 years with no real increase in cost and no diminishment in the benefits of the purchase?

An additional factor is inflation. Most of today's annuities are inadequate in protecting against inflation.[52] Maintaining control of the funds allows you to hedge the inflation risk by purchasing assets that tend to increase in inflationary periods. Annuitization is akin to purchasing a bond with amortized principal and souped-up

---

[51]DCA in general is a suboptimal investment strategy and has been shown to be mean–variance inefficient by a number of writers.

[52]Annuities are available that protect from inflation—the so-called real annuities—but they are relatively more expensive than plain annuities.

coupons. The coupons are higher than normal because the bond is completely nontransferable and goes with you to the grave. Unexpected inflation—together with a general increase in interest rates—wreaks havoc on bond prices. The same thing goes for annuities. Today's annuity products do not offer such attractive features as commutability (which would allow policyholders to withdraw cash from their immediate annuities), but the chances are good that future annuity products will.

Even though annuities are not traded in the marketplace, they lose theoretical value when interest rates increase. And all investors would do well to keep in mind that inflation is not permanently dead. In fact, the spread between yields on real and nominal bonds has been 2–3 percent in recent years. In other words, investors are expecting, roughly speaking, at least 2–3 percent inflation a year over the next 30 years. At 2 percent, $1 will be worth only half as much, in today's dollars, 30 years from now. And if a 65-year-old couple does not worry that far ahead, they should not be purchasing a life annuity in the first place.

Finally, a major reason for deferring annuitization as long as prudently possible (and perhaps even not doing so) is the bequest motive. Putting all one's money into a pure life annuity leaves nothing for one's estate. With a straight life annuity, payments cease with the buyer's death. In the worst-case scenario, which many people fear, the investor hands over $100,000 to an insurance company that promises monthly checks for the rest of the investor's life, and then, a few months later, the investor dies. The monthly checks stop coming, the rest of the $100,000 belongs to the insurance company, and the investor's estate gets nothing.[53]

The whole idea of annuity purchases involves the pooling of risk. The living are subsidized by the dying. In fact, participants in qualified retirement plans must obtain written permission from their spouses if they want to elect a single-life annuity payment. The longer someone defers annuitization, the greater the chances that the person will die prior to purchasing the life annuity, in which case, the estate inherits the proceeds of the account. Although taxes will complicate the amount, marginal tax rates are far less than 100 percent, so something will always be left over if it was not annuitized.

---

[53] If the contract has a guarantee period (which, of course, must be paid for), the monthly payments will continue until the guarantee period is over. So in this case, the estate, children, or loved ones do get something.

7. Summary and Implications

We have shown how individuals should make financial decisions throughout their lives involving more than merely asset allocation. The key to the process is the recognition that individuals have human capital as well as financial capital. This human capital contributes substantial earnings during the accumulation stage of a life cycle but should be at least partially protected with life insurance. As individuals age, human capital is depleted, but as they save, human capital is converted into financial capital. As individuals invest, this financial capital grows to replace the future consumption needs of the investor. During the retirement stage of the life cycle, the income from the human capital needs to be replaced with pensions, Social Security payments, and the returns and principal from the financial capital.

In providing an approach to making the financial decisions that individuals face, we specifically modeled personal situations in the context of the financial markets and the stock, bond, life insurance, and annuity products available to investors. Our models suggest optimal purchases of these products together with optimal financial asset allocation mixes for individuals when such variables are put in as the individuals' projected earnings stream, savings rate, retirement needs, assumed market risks and returns, and mortality tables.

Accumulation Stage

We first considered a person's accumulation stage—that is, the individual's working life, which is typically from about age 25 to age 65. The individual or family consumes part of this income and saves the rest. Saving converts human capital into financial capital. The investor faces three main risks during these years: market risk, mortality risk, and savings risk. The market risk concerns what types of returns the markets will generate on financial capital. The mortality risk concerns the potential demise of the wage earner and the resulting cessation of wage income for the family. The savings risk concerns the extent to which the individual and family are able to generate sufficient savings flow into their financial capital to adequately provide for the retirement stage of their lives.

Market risk is controlled by selecting an optimal asset allocation mix, in the context of the individual's wealth in human and financial capital, from the available products. We modeled human capital as mostly fixed and bondlike, so the optimal whole portfolio (human capital plus financial capital) requires picking only the appropriate financial asset allocation. The human capital part itself can be protected with life insurance. Finally, the savings risk is controlled by selecting an appropriate savings rate, which can be solved for.

During the accumulation stage of their lives, investors generally take their human capital as a given, although some may decide to shift their careers to meet their consumption or other financial needs. Human capital is typically a large quantity at the start of a career because it reflects the present value of all the future income that individuals are expected to earn. This human capital is bondlike (i.e., earning a relatively stable, although usually growing, and predictable income stream). Most individuals have little financial capital early in their careers. Any small amount of financial capital should be invested almost entirely in equitylike investments so that the individual's overall asset allocation (human and financial capital) has both an equity and a fixed-income component.

As individuals progress through their careers, their human capital declines. More and more of their earned income has already been achieved, and less and less of it is available for future consumption and saving. Ideally, individuals have already saved some of this income so that it will be available as part of their financial portfolio. As their financial capital becomes a greater proportion of their total wealth, financial asset allocation will begin to shift from almost all equities to a larger and larger proportion of bonds. By retirement, individuals hold most of their wealth as financial capital; therefore, the allocation of their financial assets should have a large bond component to balance the mix of their total capital.

The changes in the proportions of human capital and financial capital that occur as individuals age affect insurance needs as well as asset allocation. Early in their careers, when individuals have much human capital, protecting much of this capital with life insurance is reasonable. As individuals age, they have less human capital to protect, so less life insurance is needed. During retirement, individuals have little human capital left but some life insurance may still be desirable to ensure that a minimum level of wealth can be transferred as bequests.

During the accumulation stage, actual asset allocations and the amount of life insurance to be purchased depend not only on age but also on the progression of individual careers. These decisions depend also on the amount of financial capital that individuals have at any given time. The more financial capital an individual has, the less life insurance he or she needs to buy to protect human capital but also the more the individual needs to protect the financial capital by making conservative financial investments. If the individual is risk averse, he or she will want to protect *both* human capital and financial capital in the accumulation stage. This can be done by buying more life insurance and adding more bonds into the financial asset portfolio.

Finally, the type of work that individuals do affects their needs for life insurance and their asset allocations. Individuals who work in low-risk (bondlike) professions (e.g., tenured teachers) especially need to protect their otherwise low-risk human capital by buying sufficient life insurance. Individuals who work in careers that have earnings that are highly correlated with the stock market or the economy (e.g., stockbrokers, commissioned sales people) should view their human capital as more equitylike and attempt to reduce their overall risk by holding more bonds in their financial portfolios.

We have presented models to solve for the actual suggested amounts of life insurance that an individual (or family) should buy as well as what an investor's asset allocation mix should be throughout this accumulation stage. These models use inputs that are both specific to individual cases and marketwide. The individual-specific inputs are an individual's age, gender, family status, annual earned income, expected growth in income, the variability of the earned income, and its correlation with the stock market or risky assets in a portfolio. The inputs also include the individual's consumption, expected retirement age, pension benefits, retirement needs, risk aversion, and bequest desires. The marketwide inputs include expected returns for the stock and bond markets, their correlation with each other, their standard deviations, and estimated management fees and transaction costs in managing a portfolio. Predicted Social Security levels and structure are also inputs, together with mortality rates and life insurance fees. The outputs are the individual's suggested life insurance amounts, financial asset allocations, and savings rates.

In summary, during the accumulation stage, the following directions are suggested for individual investors:

1. The older the individual is, the less life insurance is needed and the more bonds should be included in the asset allocation.

2. The higher the initial financial wealth is, the less life insurance is needed but the more bonds should be included in the asset allocation.

3. The more risk averse an investor is, the more life insurance is needed and the more bonds should be in the asset allocation.

4. The more desire the individual has to make bequests to beneficiaries, the more life insurance is needed, but this bequest desire has little impact on asset allocation.

5. The more an individual's earning power is sensitive to the economy and the stock market, the less life insurance is needed but the more bonds are needed in the asset allocation.

Retirement Stage

After an individual reaches retirement age, most of the individual's human capital has been used up; that is, he or she will no longer be earning income on a regular basis. The individual may have a defined-benefit (DB) pension plan and Social Security benefits, and possible other sources of earned income, but much of his or her retirement consumption will probably have to be drawn from the principal and the return generated from his or her financial portfolio.

During this stage of their lives, retirees face three risks that are somewhat different from the three risks they faced in the accumulation stage. They still face market risk, probably at an even greater level than earlier because most of their capital is now financial capital. They also face longevity risk, which is the risk of outliving their assets. Finally, as they approach the end of their lives, they face a bequest risk—the risk that they may not be able to leave the desired amounts to their beneficiaries. (They may have always faced this risk, but the probabilities that they will need to make a bequest have gone up.)

Individuals control market risk by attempting to choose optimal financial asset allocations. They can control longevity risk by purchasing immediate annuities, which pay out income each year for the rest of their lives. They can collectively manage the asset allocation to include stocks, bonds, and fixed and variable annuities. Finally, they can lock in any bequests that they want to ensure by buying life insurance.

One way to meet retirement needs is to have saved sufficient amounts during the accumulation stage and invested this financial portfolio in stocks and bonds. When retirement income is needed, the investor can make systematic withdrawals from this portfolio. This procedure is likely to be successful if the investor lives to the age predicted for the person by mortality tables. Because roughly half of investors (or couples, including spouses) live past their life expectancies, however, they incur longevity risk. For long-lived investors, their systematic withdrawals from stock and bond portfolios may deplete their financial portfolios.

Not all people will have saved enough to ensure their retirement by systematically withdrawing from their stock and bond portfolios. Another way to meet retirement needs is to hedge longevity risk by purchasing immediate payout annuities. Fixed-payout annuities pay a constant stream of income for as long as the retiree lives. The fixed payout is usually expressed as a percentage of the amount of the annuity purchased. Variable-payout annuities pay out a variable stream based on the fluctuating value of an annuity portfolio so that in an up market, for example, the payout increases.

We showed how an investor can assemble a combined portfolio of stocks, bonds, and fixed-payout and variable-payout annuities. Such a portfolio can increase the probability that an individual or couple will have sufficient yearly income to maintain their standard of living throughout their life span, no matter how long they live.

A retiree is also concerned about making bequests to beneficiaries. There is always a trade-off between insuring against longevity risk and the likelihood of leaving substantial monies to beneficiaries. As in the accumulation stage, investors can ensure that bequests can be made by buying life insurance. We specifically depicted the individual's trade-off between reducing longevity risk and fulfilling bequest desires. In general, buying payout annuities reduces bequest amounts but life insurance directly protects bequests.

In putting together an optimal portfolio that includes stocks, bonds, fixed annuities, variable annuities, and life insurance, an adviser must take into account the investor's risk aversion and the returns and risk that the markets are expected to provide. Advisers can model the returns on stock and bond markets, netting out anticipated fees and transaction costs. They can do the same for the annuity products. Annuities are usually quoted net of fees, with the expected return on fixed annuities directly observable. The expected returns on variable annuities are not directly observable because the principal is expected to rise or decline with market movements.

If individuals expect Social Security payments or have a DB pension, advisers can think of them as already owning some annuities. Social Security is usually indexed to inflation, whereas pension benefits generally resemble a fixed annuity. Once a value is assigned to these existing "annuities," they can partially meet the demand for annuity products in the overall portfolio mix.

We used two types of inputs to model the optimum mix of stocks, bonds, and fixed and variable annuities. The first set of inputs came from the specific individual retiree (or couple). These included the gender, age, financial wealth, probability of living beyond their expected mortality, risk tolerance, and consumption and bequest desires. The second set of assumptions concerned the financial markets. We estimated stock and bond expected returns, standard deviations, correlation structure, and fee levels. The same was necessary, together with considering the mortality tables of the general population, for the fixed and variable annuity products.

Solving for the optimal asset allocation of stocks, bonds, and fixed and variable annuities is only part of the problem. Advisers also need to determine *when* to start purchasing annuities for a portfolio. The problem is complicated because the purchase of a payout annuity is an irreversible decision and because the transaction costs, fees, and expenses of an annuity can easily dominate the effects of mortality pooling. In addition to costs and expenses, insurance companies have to worry about the moral hazard of individuals trying to reverse their policies when they perceive that their life expectancies have shortened. For all these reasons, reversing a payout annuity entails large penalties.

So, when or at what age should an individual invest in a payout annuity? Consider the simple case of fixed-payout annuities. The rate (after costs) should exceed the fixed payments one would receive on a bond because the investor is being paid a mortality credit to cover the fact that the principal of the annuity is never repaid and the stream of income stops when the investor dies. If bequests are unimportant, then the earlier the individual invests in an annuity, the better. But most people have some bequest desires—or will develop some in the future. The irreversibility of an annuity, however, locks in the asset allocation, thus giving the investor little control if his or her circumstances change. The extreme case is premature death: The annualized income stream stops, and the annuity becomes worthless.

The benefits of annuities in reducing longevity risk diminish, however, if the individual waits too long to purchase the annuity. Given the trade-offs, we suggest waiting until after retirement to buy payout annuities and staggering the purchases.

Our models optimize the retirement asset allocation to include stocks, bonds, and fixed- and variable-payout annuities, together with sufficient life insurance to help protect the bequests that retirees want to make. Specific asset allocation findings for the retirement stage of investing are as follows:

1. Including payout annuities in a retirement asset allocation reduces the probability of outliving assets (e.g., reduces longevity risk).

2. Fixed-payout annuities substitute for bonds, and variable-payout annuities substitute for stocks, although more aggressive equity mixes can be invested in once longevity risk has been diminished.

3. Payout annuities protect against longevity risk; life insurance protects bequests that can be made. In general, the more annuities purchased, the less capital is left over for bequests.

4. Payout annuities should generally be purchased after retirement with staggered purchases because annuities are irreversible purchases that partially lock in investors' asset allocations and reduce bequests.

Modeling the Life Cycle

We have suggested ways that investors can make stock, bond, life insurance, and payout annuity decisions over their life cycles. We addressed both the accumulation stage and the retirement stage in several chapters.

The models presented here can be used to make specific recommendations. During the accumulation stage (generally from about age 25 to 65), the models can suggest optimal financial asset allocations (stock and bond mixes) and life insurance purchases. During the retirement stage, the models can suggest asset allocations to stocks, bonds, and fixed- and variable-payout annuities. When bequest desires are included, life insurance levels can also be suggested.

To implement these models for specific individuals, the adviser will need some personal information about the individuals as inputs. This information includes the investor's gender, age, family status, earnings, financial wealth, consumption and savings patterns, risk aversion, anticipated retirement age, bequest desires, and subjective life expectancy. It is also necessary for the adviser to know the expected growth and variability of the individual's earnings and the correlation of the earnings with stock and bond markets. In addition, the adviser needs to know something about the products available in the marketplace. Inputs include stock and bond expected returns, standard deviations of returns, payout annuity fixed rates, payout annuity variable expected returns and risks, costs and fees, the correlation structure among the product categories, and objective mortality rates.

Individuals face a complex set of investment decisions that continually change throughout their life cycles. We believe that research has come a long way in addressing these practical problems that investors face. We hope that the concepts and financial models presented here can help investors meet their consumption, retirement, and bequest needs.

Appendix A. Human Capital and the Asset Allocation Model

The term "human capital" often conveys a number of different and, at times, conflicting ideas in the insurance, economics, and finance literature. We define human capital as "the financial, economic present value of net incomes that depend on a number of subjective or market pricing factors." In general, the net incomes are wages or salaries before retirement and pension payments after retirement.

Measuring the Present Value of Human Capital

Let the symbol h_t denote the random (real, after-tax) income that a person will receive during the discrete time period (or year) t; then, in general, the expected discounted value of this income flow, $DVHC$, at the current time, t_0, is represented mathematically by

$$DVHC = \sum_{t=1}^{n} \frac{E[h_t]}{(1+r+v)^t},$$ (A.1)

where n is the number of periods over which we are discounting, r is the relevant risk-free discount rate, and v is a (subjective) parameter that captures illiquidity plus any other potential risk premium associated with one's human capital. In Equation A.1, the expectation $E[h_t]$ in the numerator converts the random income into a scalar. Note that in addition to expectations (under a physical, real-world measure) in Equation A.1, the denominator's v, which accounts for all broadly defined risks, obviously reduces the t_0 value of the expression $DVHC$ accordingly.

And depending on the investor's specific job and profession, he or she might be expected to earn the same exact $E[h_t]$ in each time period t, yet the random shocks to incomes, $h_t - E[h_t]$, might have very different statistical characteristics vis-à-vis the market portfolio; thus, each profession or job will induce a distinct "risk premium" value for v, which will then lead to a lower discounted expected value of human capital. Therefore, because we are discounting with an explicit risk premium, we feel justified in also using the term "financial economic value of human capital" to describe $DVHC$.

Similarly, in the discussions in Chapters 2 and 3, when we focus on the correlation or covariance between human capital and other macroeconomic or financial factors, we are, of course, referring to the correlation between shocks $h_t - E[h_t]$

and shocks to or innovations in the return-generating process in the market. This correlation can induce a (quite complicated) dependence structure between *DVHC* in Equation A.1 and the dynamic evolution of the investor's financial portfolio.[54]

Model Specification: Optimal Asset Allocation with Human Capital

We assume that the investor is currently age x and will retire at age y. The term "retirement" is simply meant to indicate that the human capital income flow is terminated and the pension phase begins. We further assume that the financial portfolio will be rebalanced annually. We do not consider taxes in our models. The investor would like to know what fraction of his or her financial wealth should be invested in a risky asset (stock).

In the model, an investor determines the allocation to the risky asset, α_x, to maximize the year-end utility of total wealth (human capital plus financial wealth). The optimization problem can be expressed as

$$\max_{(\alpha_x)} E\left[U\left(W_{x+1} + H_{x+1}\right)\right], \tag{A.2}$$

subject to the budget constraints

$$W_{x+1} = \left(W_x + h_x - C_x\right)\left[\alpha_x e^{\mu_S - (1/2)\sigma_S^2 + \sigma_S Z_S} + (1 - \alpha_x)e^{r_f}\right], \tag{A.3}$$

where e is the exponent, 2.7182, and

$$0 \le \alpha_x \le 1. \tag{A.4}$$

The symbols, notations, and terminology used in the optimal problem are as follows:

α_x = allocation to the risky asset.

W_t = financial wealth at time t. The market has two assets—one risky and one risk free. This assumption is consistent with the two-fund separation theorem of traditional portfolio theory. Of course, the approach could be expanded to multiple asset classes.

r_f = return on the risk-free asset.

S_t = value of the risky asset at time t. This value follows a discrete version of a geometric Brownian motion:

$$S_{t+1} = S_t \exp\left(\mu_S - \frac{1}{2}\sigma_S^2 + \sigma_S Z_{S,t+1}\right), \tag{A.5}$$

---

[54]For a more rigorous and mathematically satisfying treatment of the ongoing interaction between human capital and market returns as it pertains to the purchase of life insurance in a continuous-time framework, see Huang, Milevsky, and Wang (2005).

where μ_S is the expected return and σ_S is the standard deviation of return of the risky asset. $Z_{S,t}$ is a random variable. $Z_{S,t} \sim N(0,1)$.

h_t = value of labor income. In our numerical cases, we assume that h_t follows a discrete stochastic process specified by

$$h_{t+1} = h_t \exp\left(\mu_h + \sigma_h Z_{h,t+1}\right),$$ (A.6)

where $h_t > 0$; μ_h and σ_h are, respectively, the annual growth rate and the annual standard deviation of the income process and $Z_{h,t}$ is a random variable. $Z_{h,t} \sim N(0,1)$.

Based on Equation A.6, for a person at age x, income at age $x + t$ is determined by

$$h_{x+t} = h_x \left[\prod_{k=1}^{t} \exp\left(\mu_h + \sigma_h Z_{h,k}\right)\right].$$ (A.7)

We further assume that correlation between labor income innovation and the return of the risky asset is ρ. That is,

$$\mathrm{corr}(Z_S, Z_h) = \rho.$$ (A.8)

Mathematically, the relationship between Z_S and Z_h can be expressed as

$$Z_h = \rho Z_S + \sqrt{1-\rho^2}\, Z,$$ (A.9)

where Z is a standard Brownian motion independent of Z_S and Z_h.

H_t = value of human capital at time t. It is the present value of future income from age $t + 1$ to life expectancy. Income after retirement is the payment from pensions.

Based on Equation A.7, for a person at age $x + t$, the present value of future income from age $x + t + 1$ to life expectancy, denoted as T, is determined by

$$H_{x+t} = \sum_{j=t+1}^{T} \left\{h_{x+j}\exp\left[-(j-t)(r_f + \eta_h + \zeta_h)\right]\right\},$$ (A.10)

where η_h is the risk premium (discount rate) for the income process and captures the market risk of income and ζ_h is a discount factor in human capital evaluation to account for the illiquidity risk associated with one's job. We assumed a 4 percent discount rate per year.[55]

---

[55]The 4 percent discount rate translates into about a 25 percent discount on the overall present value of human capital for a 45-year-old with 20 years of future salary. This 25 percent discount is consistent with empirical evidence on the discount factor between restricted stocks and their unrestricted counterparts (e.g., Amihud and Mendelson 1991). Also, Longstaff (2002) reported that the liquidity premium for the longer-maturity U.S. T-bond is 10–15 percent of the value of the bond.

Based on the capital asset pricing model, η_h can be evaluated by

$$\eta_h = \frac{\text{cov}(Z_h, Z_S)}{\text{var}(Z_S)}(\mu_S - r_f)$$

$$= \rho\left[\mu_S - \left(e^{r_f} - 1\right)\right]\frac{\sigma_h}{\sigma_S}. \tag{A.11}$$

Furthermore, the expected value of H_t, which is $E[H_{x+t}]$, is defined as the human capital a person has at age $x + t + 1$.

C_t = consumption in year t. For simplicity, C_t is assumed to equal C (i.e., constant consumption over time).

The power utility function (constant relative risk aversion) is used in our numerical examples. The functional form of the utility function is

$$U(W) = \frac{W^{1-\gamma}}{1-\gamma} \tag{A.12}$$

for $W \geq 0$ and $\gamma \neq 1$ and

$$U(W) = \ln(W) \tag{A.13}$$

for $W \geq 0$ and $\gamma = 1$. The power utility function is used in the examples for $U(\cdot)$.

We solved the problem via simulation. We first simulated the values of the risky asset by using Equation A.5. Then, we simulated Z_h from Equation A.9 to take into account the correlation between income change and return from the financial market. Finally, we used Equation A.6 to generate income over the same period. Human capital, H_{x+t}, was calculated by using Equations A.7 and A.10. If wealth level at age $x + 1$ was less than zero, we set the wealth equal to zero; that is, we assumed that the investor had no remaining financial wealth. We simulated this process N times. The objective function was evaluated by using

$$\frac{1}{N}\sum_{n=1}^{N} U[W_{x+1}(n) + H_{x+1}(n)]. \tag{A.14}$$

In the numerical examples, we set N equal to 20,000.

Appendix B. Life Insurance and the Asset Allocation Model

We describe here the basic pricing mechanism of life insurance and, more importantly, provide the detailed model that underlies the numerical results and examples in Chapter 3.

Pricing Mechanism for One-Year, Renewable Term Life Insurance

The one-year renewable term policy *premium* is paid at the beginning of the year and protects the human capital of the insured for the duration of the year. (If the insured person dies within that year, the insurance company pays the *face value* to the beneficiaries soon after the death or prior to the end of the year.) In the next year, the contract is guaranteed to start anew with new premium payments to be made and protection received; hence the word "renewable."

The policy premium is obviously an increasing function of the desired face value, and the two are related by the following simple formula:

$$P = \frac{q}{1+r}\theta. \tag{B.1}$$

The premium, P, is calculated by multiplying the desired face value, θ, by the probability of death, q, and then discounted by the interest rate factor, $1 + r$. The theory behind Equation B.1 is the well-known *law of large numbers*, which guarantees that probabilities become percentages when individual probabilities are aggregated. Note the implicit assumption in Equation B.1: Although death can occur at any time during the year (or term), the premium payments are made at the beginning of the year, and the face values are paid at the end of the year. From the insurance company's perspective, all of the premiums received from the group of N individuals of the same age (i.e., having the same probability of death) are commingled and invested in an *insurance reserve* earning a rate of interest r so that at the end of the year, $PN(1 + r)$ is divided among the qN beneficiaries.

No savings component or investment component is embedded in the premium defined by Equation B.1. To the contrary, at the end of the year, the survivor loses any claim to the pool of accumulated premiums because all funds go directly to the beneficiaries.

As the individual ages, his or her probability of death increases (denoted by adding the subscript x to the probability, q_x). In this case, the same face amount (face value) of life insurance, θ, will cost more and will induce a higher premium, P_x, per Equation B.1. Note that in practice, the actual premium is *loaded* by an additional factor, $1 + \lambda$, to account for commissions, transaction costs, and profit margins. So, the actual amount paid by the insured is closer to $P(1 + \lambda)$, but the underlying pricing relationship driven by the law of large numbers remains the same.

Also, from a traditional financial planning perspective, the individual conducts a budgeting analysis to determine his or her life insurance demands (i.e., the amount the surviving family and beneficiaries need, in present value terms, in order to replace wages lost as a result of death). That quantity is taken as the required face value in Equation B.1, which then produces a premium. Alternatively, one can think of a budget for life insurance purchases, and the face value is then determined by Equation B.1.

In our model and the related discussion, we "solve" for the optimal age-varying amount of life insurance, θ_x (which then provides the age-varying policy payment, P_x), that maximizes the welfare of the family by taking into account the investor's or family's risk preferences and attitudes toward leaving a bequest as well as replacing lost income.

Model Specification: Optimal Asset Allocation, Human Capital, and Insurance Demands

The model specification in Chapter 3 is an extension of the model of optimal asset allocation with human capital provided in Appendix A and discussed in Chapter 2.

We start with assuming that the investor is currently age x and will retire at age Y. The term "retirement" as we use it here is simply meant to indicate that the income flow from human capital terminates and the pension phase begins. We further assume that the financial portfolio will be rebalanced annually and that the life insurance—which is assumed to be the one-year, renewable term policy—will be renewed annually. (We do not consider taxes in our models.)

In the model, the investor determines the amount of life insurance to demand, θ_x (that is, the face value of the policy, or "death benefit"), together with the allocation to the risky asset, α_x, that will maximize the year-end utility of the investor's total wealth (human capital plus financial wealth) weighted by the "alive" and "dead" states. The optimization problem can be expressed as

$$\max_{(\theta_x,\, \alpha_x)} E\left[(1-D)(1-\bar{q}_x)U_{alive}\left(W_{x+1}+H_{x+1}\right)+D\left(\bar{q}_x\right)U_{dead}\left(W_{x+1}+\theta_x\right)\right], \quad \text{(B.2)}$$

which is Equation 3.1 in Chapter 3, subject to the following budget constraints:

$$W_{x+1}=\left[W_x+h_x-(1+\lambda)q_x\theta_x e^{-r_f}-C_x\right]\left[\alpha_x e^{\mu_S-(1/2)\sigma_S^2+\sigma_S Z_S}+(1-\alpha_x)e^{r_f}\right], \quad \text{(B.3)}$$

$$\theta_0 \le \theta_x \le \frac{(W_x + h_x - C_x)e^{r_f}}{(1+\lambda)q_x}, \tag{B.4}$$

and

$$0 \le \alpha_x \le 1. \tag{B.5}$$

Equation B.4 requires the cost (or price) of the term insurance policy to be less than the amount of the client's current financial wealth, and the investor is required to purchase a minimum insurance amount ($\theta_0 > 0$) in order to have minimum protection from the loss of human capital. The symbols, notations, and terminology used in the optimal problem are as follows:

θ_x = face value or death benefit of life insurance.

α_x = allocation to risky assets.

D = relative strength of the utility of bequest. Individuals with no utility of bequest will have $D = 0$.

q_x = *objective* probability of death at the end of the year $x + 1$ conditional on being alive at age x. It is used in pricing insurance contracts.

$\bar{q}_x$ = *subjective* probability of death at the end of the year $x + 1$ conditional on being alive at age x; $1 - \bar{q}_x$ denotes the subjective probability of survival. The subjective probability of death may be different from the objective probability. In other words, a person might believe he or she is healthier (or less healthy) than population average. This belief would affect expected utility but not the pricing of the life insurance, which is based on an objective population survival probability.

λ = fees and expenses (i.e., actuarial and insurance loading) imposed and charged on a typical life insurance policy.

W_t = financial wealth at time t. The market has two assets—one risky and one risk free. This assumption is consistent with the two-fund separation theorem of traditional portfolio theory. Of course, the approach could be expanded to multiple asset classes.

r_f = return on the risk-free asset.

S_t = value of the risky asset. This value follows a discrete version of a geometric Brownian motion:

$$S_{t+1} = S_t \exp\left(\mu_S - \frac{1}{2}\sigma_S^2 + \sigma_S Z_{S,t+1}\right), \tag{B.6}$$

where μ_S is the expected return, σ_S is the standard deviation of return of the risky asset, and $Z_{S,t}$ is a random variable; $Z_{S,t} \sim N(0,1)$.

h_t = value of labor income. In our numerical cases, we assume that h_t follows a discrete stochastic process specified by

$$h_{t+1} = h_t \exp(\mu_h + \sigma_h Z_{h,t+1}), \tag{B.7}$$

where $h_t > 0$; μ_h and σ_h are, respectively, the annual growth rate and the annual standard deviation of the income process; and $Z_{h,t}$ is a random variable. $Z_{h,t} \sim N(0,1)$.

Based on Equation B.7, for a person at age x, income at age $x + t$ is determined by

$$h_{x+t} = h_x \left[\prod_{k=1}^{t} \exp\left(\mu_h + \sigma_h Z_{h,k}\right) \right]. \tag{B.8}$$

ρ = correlation between changes in labor income and the return of the risky asset; that is,

$$\mathrm{corr}(Z_S, Z_h) = \rho. \tag{B.9}$$

Mathematically, the relationship between Z_S and Z_h can be expressed as

$$Z_h = \rho Z_S + \sqrt{1 - \rho^2}\, Z, \tag{B.10}$$

where Z is a standard Brownian motion independent of Z_S and Z_h.

H_t = human capital value at time t. It is the present value of future income from age $t + 1$ to life expectancy. Income after retirement is the payment from pensions.

Based on Equation B.8, for a person at age $x + t$, the present value of future income from age $x + t + 1$ to life expectancy denoted as T is determined by

$$H_{x+t} = \sum_{j=t+1}^{T} \left\{ h_{x+j} \exp\left[-(j-t)(r_f + \eta_h + \zeta_h)\right] \right\}, \tag{B.11}$$

where η_h is the risk premium (discount rate) for the income process and captures the market risk of income and ζ_h is a discount factor in human capital evaluation to account for the illiquidity risk associated with one's job. In the numerical examples, we assume a 4 percent discount rate per year.[56]

Based on the capital asset pricing model, η_h can be evaluated by

$$\eta_h = \frac{\mathrm{cov}(Z_h, Z_S)}{\mathrm{var}(Z_S)} \left[\mu_S - \left(e^{r_f} - 1\right) \right]$$

$$= \rho \left[\mu_S - \left(e^{r_f} - 1\right) \right] \frac{\sigma_h}{\sigma_S}. \tag{B.12}$$

---

[56] See the discussion of this issue in Appendix A.

Furthermore, the expected value of H_t, which is $E(H_{x+t})$, is defined as the human capital a person has at age $x + t + 1$.

C_t = consumption in year t. For simplicity, C_t is assumed to equal C (i.e., constant consumption over time).

The power utility function (constant relative risk aversion) is used in our numerical examples. The functional form of the utility function is

$$U(W) = \frac{W^{1-\gamma}}{1-\gamma} \tag{B.13}$$

for $W \geq 0$ and $\gamma \neq 1$ and

$$U(W) = \ln(W) \tag{B.14}$$

for $W \geq 0$ and $\gamma = 1$. The power utility function is used in the examples for both $U_{alive}(\cdot)$ and $U_{dead}(\cdot)$, which are the utility functions associated with, respectively, the alive and dead states.

We solved the problem via simulation. We first simulated the values of the risky asset by using Equation B.6. Then, we simulated Z_h from Equation B.10 to take into account the correlation between income change and return from the financial market. Finally, we used Equation B.7 to generate income over the same period. Human capital, H_{x+t}, was calculated by using Equations B.8 and B.11. If wealth level at age $x + 1$ was less than zero, then we set the wealth equal to zero; that is, we assumed that the investor has no remaining financial wealth. We simulated this process N times. The objective function was evaluated by using

$$\frac{1}{N} \sum_{n=1}^{N} U_{alive} \left[W_{x+1}(n) + H_{x+1}(n) \right] \tag{B.15}$$

and

$$\frac{1}{N} \sum_{n=1}^{N} U_{dead} \left[W_{x+1}(n) + \theta_x \right]. \tag{B.16}$$

In the numerical examples, we set N equal to 20,000.

Appendix C. Payout Annuity Variations

Chapter 4 describes the two basic types of payout annuities—fixed and variable. In this appendix, we discuss some variations in payout annuities.

Single-Life and Joint-Life Annuities

When considering retirement security, retirees must consider the retirement income needs of their spouses. For example, if a married couple converts their savings into a single-life payout annuity on the husband, then at his death, the wife will experience a 100 percent decline in annuity income. This issue can be solved by purchasing joint-life annuities.

A joint-life annuity is structured to provide income for as long as either member of a couple is alive. Because a joint-life payout annuity makes payments much longer, on average, than a single-life payout annuity, the joint option reduces the income payment each year. Depending on the couple's preferences, the annuity can be designed to provide the same income after the death of a spouse or provide a reduced level of income.

Table C.1 illustrates the difference in terms of payments for a fixed-payout annuity for a single-life annuity for a man, a single-life annuity for a woman, and a joint payout with 100 percent survivor benefit. The payment amount is calculated for an initial premium or purchase amount of $100,000. For a 65-year-old man, the payment would be $654 per month. For a 65-year-old woman, the payment would be $616 per month. For a joint payout with 100 percent survivor benefit, the payment would fall to $6,492 per year.

Table C.1. Immediate Fixed-Payout Annuity Payments

Payment	Single Male	Single Female	Joint
Annual payment	$7,848	$7,392	$6,492

Note: Initial premium or purchase amount of $100,000; age 65 years for male and female.

Source: Ibbotson Associates, based on industry quotes in June 2005.

Payment-Period Guarantees

Another variation in annuitization is payment-period guarantees. Some retirees who wish to purchase annuities may be concerned that early death could result in only a short period of annuity payment. These retirees would like a portion of their original premium payment to be made available to their heirs. This arrangement can be achieved by purchasing payout annuities with payment-period guarantees. These guarantees provide a minimum number of monthly payments regardless of the age of the annuitant's death or offer a partial return of premium at death.

Choosing a guarantee period decreases the amount of income paid out each period to the retiree. **Table C.2** presents a comparison of the payment differences for no guarantee in the contract, for a 10-year guarantee period, and for a 20-year guarantee period.

Table C.2. Immediate Fixed-Payout Annuities with Period Guarantees

Guarantee Period	Single Male	Single Female	Joint
No guarantee	$7,848	$7,392	$6,492
10-year guarantee	7,584	7,236	6,492
20-year guarantee	6,960	6,828	6,360

Note: Initial premium or purchase amount of $100,000; age 65 years for male and female.

Source: Ibbotson Associates, based on industry quotes in June 2005.

Guaranteed Payment Floors

Guaranteed payment floors may be added to immediate variable annuities. They guarantee that the monthly payment will not drop below a certain percentage of the first payment (for example, 80 percent). The goal is to provide a minimum monthly payment without giving up the potential increase in payments provided by a variable annuity. A guaranteed minimum income benefit is typically offered as an optional feature or rider to a variable annuity contract for an additional charge, generally ranging from 0.30 percent to 0.75 percent of the contract's account value.

References

Ameriks, John, and Stephen Zeldes. 2001. "How Do Household Portfolio Shares Vary with Age?" Working paper, Columbia University.

Ameriks, John, Robert Veres, and Mark J. Warshawsky. 2001. "Making Retirement Income Last a Lifetime." *Journal of Financial Planning*, Article 6 (December): www.journalfp.net.

Amihud, Yakov, and Haim Mendelson. 1991. "Liquidity, Asset Prices, and Financial Policy." *Financial Analysts Journal*, vol. 47, no. 6 (November/December):56–66.

Auerbach, Alan J., and Laurence Kotlikoff. 1991. "Life Insurance Inadequacy— Evidence from a Sample of Older Widows." NBER Working Paper 3765 (July).

Benartzi, Shlomo. 2001. "Excessive Extrapolation and the Allocation of 401(k) Accounts to Company Stock." *Journal of Finance*, vol. 56, no. 5:1747–1764.

Benartzi, Shlomo, and Richard H. Thaler. 2001. "Naive Diversification Strategies in Defined Contribution Saving Plans." *American Economic Review*, vol. 91, no. 1 (March):79–98.

Bengen, William P. 2001. "Conserving Client Portfolios during Retirement, Part IV." *Journal of Financial Planning*, Article 14 (May): www.journalfp.net.

Bernheim, B. Douglas. 1991. "How Strong Are Bequest Motives? Evidence Based on Estimates of the Demand for Life Insurance and Annuities." *Journal of Political Economy*, vol. 99, no. 5 (October):899–927.

Blake, David, Andrew J.G. Cairns, and Kevin Dowd. 2000. "PensionMetrics: Stochastic Pension Plan Design during the Distribution Phase." Working paper, Pensions Institute (November).

Bodie, Zvi, Robert C. Merton, and William F. Samuelson. 1992. "Labor Supply Flexibility and Portfolio Choice in a Life Cycle Model." *Journal of Economic Dynamics and Control*, vol. 16, nos. 3–4 (July/October):427–449.

Brown, J.R. 2001. "Private Pensions, Mortality Risk, and the Decision to Annuitize." *Journal of Public Economics*, vol. 82, no. 1 (October):29–62.

Brown, J.R., and J. Poterba. 2000. "Joint Life Annuities and Annuity Demand by Married Couples." *Journal of Risk and Insurance*, vol. 67, no. 4 (December):527–553.

Brown, J.R., and M.J. Warshawsky. 2001. "Longevity-Insured Retirement Distributions from Pension Plans: Market and Regulatory Issues." NBER Working Paper 8064.

Browne, S., Moshe A. Milevsky, and T.S. Salisbury. 2003. "Asset Allocation and the Liquidity Premium for Illiquid Annuities." *Journal of Risk and Insurance*, vol. 70, no. 3 (September):509–526.

Brugiavini, Agar. 1993. "Uncertainty Resolution and the Timing of Annuity Purchases." *Journal of Public Economics*, vol. 50, no. 1 (January):31–62.

Buser, Stephen A., and Michael L. Smith. 1983. "Life Insurance in a Portfolio Context." *Insurance, Mathematics & Economics*, vol. 2, no. 3:147–157.

Campbell, Ritchie A. 1980. "The Demand for Life Insurance: An Application of the Economics of Uncertainty." *Journal of Finance*, vol. 35, no. 5 (December):1155–1172.

Campbell, John, and Luis Viceira. 2002. *Strategic Asset Allocation—Portfolio Choice for Long-Term Investors*. New York: Oxford University Press.

Chen, Peng, and Moshe A. Milevsky. 2003. "Merging Asset Allocation and Longevity Insurance: An Optimal Perspective on Payout Annuities." *Journal of Financial Planning*, vol. 16, no. 6 (June):52–62.

Chen, Peng, Roger G. Ibbotson, Moshe A. Milevsky, and Kevin X. Zhu. 2006. "Human Capital, Asset Allocation, and Life Insurance." *Financial Analysts Journal*, vol. 62, no. 1 (January/February):97–109.

Davidoff, Thomas, Jeffrey R. Brown, and Peter A. Diamond. 2005. "Annuities and Individual Welfare." *American Economic Review*, vol. 95, no. 5 (December): 1573–1590.

Davis, Stephen J., and Paul Willen. 2000. "Occupation-Level Income Shocks and Asset Returns: Their Covariance and Implications for Portfolio Choice." Working paper, University of Chicago Graduate School of Business.

EBRI. 2000. "Retirement Confidence Survey." Washington, DC: Employee Benefit Research Institute.

———. 2001. "Retirement Confidence Survey." Washington, DC: Employee Benefit Research Institute.

———. 2006. "Retirement Confidence Survey." Washington, DC: Employee Benefit Research Institute.

Economides, Nicholas. 1982. "Demand for Life Insurance: An Application of the Economics of Uncertainty: A Comment." *Journal of Finance*, vol. 37, no. 5 (December):1305–1309.

Federal Reserve Board. 2004. "Survey of Consumer Finances" (www.norc.org/projects/scf/homepage.htm).

Fischer, S. 1973. "A Life Cycle Model of Life Insurance Purchases." *International Economic Review*, vol. 14, no. 1 (February):132–152.

GAO. 2003. "Report to Congressional Requesters: Private Pensions." U.S. General Accounting Office (July): www.gao.gov/new.items/d03810.pdf.

Gokhale, Jagadeesh, and Laurence J. Kotlikoff. 2002. "The Adequacy of Life Insurance." *Research Dialogue*, no. 72 (July): www.tiaa-crefinstitute.org.

Hanna, Sherman, and Peng Chen. 1997. "Subjective and Objective Risk Tolerance: Implications for Optimal Portfolios." *Financial Counseling and Planning*, vol. 8, no. 2:17–25.

Heaton, John, and Deborah Lucas. 1997. "Market Frictions, Savings Behavior, and Portfolio Choice." *Macroeconomic Dynamics*, vol. 1, no. 1 (March):76–101.

———. 2000. "Portfolio Choice and Asset Prices: The Importance of Entrepreneurial Risk." *Journal of Finance*, vol. 55, no. 3 (June):1163–1198.

Huang, H., A. Moshe Milevsky, and Jin Wang. 2005. "Portfolio Choice and Life Insurance." Research report, IFID Centre (September): www.ifid.ca.

Ibbotson Associates. 2006. *Stocks, Bonds, Bills, and Inflation 2006 Yearbook*. Chicago: Ibbotson Associates.

Ibbotson, Roger G., and Paul D. Kaplan. 2000. "Does Asset Allocation Policy Explain 40, 90, or 100 Percent of Performance?" *Financial Analysts Journal*, vol. 56, no. 1 (January/February):26–33.

Jagannathan, Ravi, and N.R. Kocherlakota. 1996. "Why Should Older People Invest Less in Stocks Than Younger People?" *Federal Reserve Bank of Minneapolis Quarterly Review*, vol. 20, no. 3 (Summer):11–23.

Kapur, Sandeep, and J. Michael Orszag. 1999. "A Portfolio Approach to Investment and Annuitization during Retirement." Mimeo, Birkbeck College, London (May).

Lee, Hye Kyung, and Sherman Hanna. 1995. "Investment Portfolios and Human Wealth." *Financial Counseling and Planning*, vol. 6:147–152.

Longstaff, Francis A. 2002. "The Flight-to-Liquidity Premium in U.S. Treasury Bond Prices." NBER Working Paper 9312 (November).

Malkiel, Burton G. 2004. *A Random Walk Down Wall Street*. 8th ed. New York: Norton & Company.

Markowitz, Harry M. 1952. "Portfolio Selection." *Journal of Finance*, vol. 7, no. 1 (March):77–91.

———. 1990. *Portfolio Selection*. 2nd ed. Oxford, U.K.: Blackwell Publishers.

Merton, Robert C. 1969. "Lifetime Portfolio Selection under Uncertainty: The Continuous-Time Case." *Review of Economics and Statistics*, vol. 51, no. 3 (August):247–257.

———. 1971. "Optimum Consumption and Portfolio Rules in a Continuous-Time Model." *Journal of Economic Theory*, vol. 3, no. 4 (December):373–413.

———. 2003. "Thoughts on the Future: Theory and Practice in Investment Management." *Financial Analysts Journal*, vol. 59, no. 1 (January/February):17–23.

Meulbroek, Lisa. 2002. "Company Stock in Pension Plans: How Costly Is It?" Working Paper 02-058, Harvard Business School (March).

Milevsky, Moshe A. 2001. "Spending Your Retirement in Monte Carlo." *Journal of Retirement Planning*, vol. 4 (January/February):21–29.

———. 2005a. "Advanced Life Delayed Annuities: Pure Longevity Insurance with Deductibles." *North American Actuarial Journal*, vol. 9, no. 4 (October):109–122.

———. 2005b. "The Implied Longevity Yield: A Note on Developing an Index for Payout Annuities." *Journal of Risk and Insurance*, vol. 72, no. 2 (June):301–320.

Milevsky, Moshe A., and Anna Abaimova. 2005. "Variable Payout Annuities with Downside Protection: How to Replace the Lost Longevity Insurance in DC Plans." Research report, IFID Centre (October): www.ifid.ca.

Milevsky, Moshe A., and Chris Robinson. 2005. "A Sustainable Spending Rate without Simulation." *Financial Analysts Journal*, vol. 61, no. 6 (November/December):89–100.

Milevsky, Moshe A., and Virginia R. Young. 2002. "Optimal Asset Allocation and the Real Option to Delay Annuitization: It's Not Now-or-Never." Pensions Institute Working Paper 0211 (September): www.pensions-institute.org/workingpapers/wp0211.pdf.

———. 2007. "Annuitization and Asset Allocation." *Journal of Economic Dynamics and Control* (http://linkinghub.elsevier.com/retrieve/pii/S0165188906002041).

Milevsky, Moshe A., Kristen Moore, and Virginia R. Young. 2006. "Asset Allocation and Annuity-Purchase Strategies to Minimize the Probability of Financial Ruin." *Mathematical Finance*, vol. 16, no. 4 (October):647–671.

Mitchell, Olivia S., James M. Poterba, Mark J. Warshawsky, and Jeffrey R. Brown. 1999. "New Evidence on the Money's Worth of Individual Annuities." *American Economic Review*, vol. 89, no. 5 (December):1299–1318.

Ostaszewski, Krzysztof. 2003. "Is Life Insurance a Human Capital Derivatives Business?" *Journal of Insurance Issues*, vol. 26, no. 1:1–14.

Poterba, James. 1997. "The History of Annuities in the United States." NBER Working Paper 6001 (April).

Richard, Scott F. 1975. "Optimal Consumption, Portfolio and Life Insurance Rules for an Uncertain Lived Individual in a Continuous Time Model." *Journal of Financial Economics*, vol. 2, no. 2 (June):187–203.

Samuelson, Paul A. 1969. "Lifetime Portfolio Selection by Dynamic Stochastic Programming." *Review of Economics and Statistics*, vol. 51, no. 3 (August):239–246.

Thaler, Richard, and Shlomo Benartzi. 2004. "Save More Tomorrow: Using Behavioral Economics to Increase Employee Savings." *Journal of Political Economy*, vol. 112, no. 1, Part 2 (February):S164–S187.

Todd, Jerry D. 2004. "Integrative Life Insurance Needs Analysis." *Journal of Financial Service Professionals* (March).

Yaari, M.E. 1965. "Uncertain Lifetime, Life Insurance, and the Theory of the Consumer." *Review of Economic Studies*, vol. 32, no. 2 (April):137–150.

Yagi, T., and Y. Nishigaki. 1993. "The Inefficiency of Private Constant Annuities." *Journal of Risk and Insurance*, vol. 60, no. 3 (September):385–412.

Zietz, Emily N. 2003. "An Examination of the Demand for Life Insurance." *Risk Management & Insurance Review*, vol. 6, no. 2 (September):159–191.